Called to Serve

Called to Serve

Stories of Atlantic Baptist Women in Ministry

EDITED BY HANNAH HUNT,
JOETTA FERNANDO,
AND MELODY MAXWELL

Foreword by Renée MacVicar

WIPF & STOCK • Eugene, Oregon

CALLED TO SERVE
Stories of Atlantic Baptist Women in Ministry

Wipf & Stock
An Imprint of Wipf and Stock Publishers
199 W. 8th Ave., Suite 3
Eugene, OR 97401

www.wipfandstock.com

PAPERBACK ISBN: 979-8-3852-6279-3
HARDCOVER ISBN: 979-8-3852-6280-9
EBOOK ISBN: 979-8-3852-6281-6

VERSION NUMBER 030426

Dedicated to all of the courageous women we've interviewed through Called to Serve

"The Lord announces the word, and the women who proclaim it are a mighty throng."

—Psalm 68:11 (NIV)

Contents

Foreword

RENÉE MACVICAR

Executive Minister, Canadian Baptists of Atlantic Canada

For more than seventy years, God has been calling women within the Atlantic Baptist family to serve, to preach, to shepherd, and to lead in Jesus' name. And for more than seventy years, courageous women have said yes.

When Josephine Kinley Moore was ordained in 1954, she stepped into a role many said was impossible for a woman to hold. Her courage, faithfulness, and obedience opened the door for others to follow. The 1987 Atlantic Baptist assembly's affirmation of allowing churches to present female candidates for ordination was another Spirit-led step forward, recognizing that the gifts of the Spirit are not limited by gender, culture, or generation. Generations of women since then have stepped forward to preach the gospel, plant and lead churches, serve as missionaries, offer chaplaincy and pastoral care, build ministries in communities across Atlantic Canada, and carry the hope of Christ into neighbourhoods across our world.

This book and the entire Called to Serve project are a gift to all of us. They capture stories that could so easily have been lost: the lived experiences, the struggles, the joys, and the steadfast obedience of women who ministered when the path was uncertain.

I am deeply grateful that these stories will now be preserved, celebrated, and passed on. As you read these pages, moments of Atlantic Baptist history will come to life—moments of challenge, breakthrough, heartbreak, and joy.

These are stories of women who broke ground. Women who stayed. Women who persevered. Women who chose faithfulness in seasons when faithfulness demanded everything from them. And woven through each story is the faithfulness of God.

As I write this foreword, I do so not only as the Executive Minister of the Canadian Baptists of Atlantic Canada (CBAC), humbled to be the first woman to serve in this role, but also as someone whose own story was shaped by those who came before me. I stand where I do today because faithful women—and faithful churches of men and women—made room, lifted me up, and believed that God's call is for all of us. Thank you; our stories are your stories too.

I think of two of the women whose stories appear in this book: Sherrolyn Riley, who persevered through injustice and discouragement, and found new joy and belonging in a congregation who grew to love her deeply; and Sandra Sutherland, whose pastoral care, love for children, and spiritual direction have helped many discover God's healing presence and leading. I also call to mind two women featured on the *Called to Serve* podcast: Lois McLean, whose steadfast faith and gentle strength shaped generations through her ministry and personal mentorship; and Dr. Anna Robbins, whose academic leadership, preaching, and theological clarity have influenced not only the CBAC but also Baptists across Canada and around the world. These women's courage, faith, and obedience have shaped my ministry more than they may ever know.

This book matters because stories matter. Stories make space for others to imagine what God might do in and through them. Stories help us recognize what the Spirit is doing among *us*. Stories help us believe that God's hope is active in us and in our day. The women in these pages did not set out to become "firsts," "pioneers," or "examples." They simply followed Jesus. But in doing so, they became role models for all of us, showing what it looks like to trust God, serve faithfully, hold on to hope, and *overflow* with hope.

To every woman whose story has been shared through this project: thank you. Your ministries have shaped congregations, communities, and people across Atlantic Canada and far beyond. Your leadership has formed a legacy that will strengthen followers of Jesus and churches into the future. Your courage has made it possible for people like me to answer God's call with boldness and joy.

As you, the reader, encounter these stories, I hope you hear not just the experiences of these remarkable women, but the invitation of the Spirit. Every generation must decide again to say yes to God's calling. Every congregation must choose to make room for the gifts of all God's people.

And so, I offer this challenge: if God is calling you—man or woman, young or old—to ministry: say yes. Trust God's voice.

And if you see someone around you discerning God's call, please encourage them. Champion them. Pray for them. Create space for them. Give them opportunities. Help them flourish.

Our churches and our world need women and men who will courageously follow God and who will support and bless those who are stepping into God's call today.

I am deeply grateful for this project and excited for the impact it will have in the years ahead. May these stories inspire you, challenge you, and fill you with hope.

Acknowledgments

THIS BOOK AND THE CALLED TO SERVE project would not have been possible without the efforts of many individuals. First and foremost, we thank the more than one hundred women in ministry whom we interviewed. Their stories have blessed and challenged us, demonstrating their obedience to God's call throughout a variety of circumstances. We are especially grateful to the fourteen women who have allowed us to share their stories in this volume. We also appreciate the efforts of the research assistants who have worked on Called to Serve within the past several years: Taylor Adams, Taylore Anstey, Samantha Diotte, and Melissa Hodder. For their generous funding that has made our project possible, we extend gratitude to the Social Sciences and Humanities Research Council of Canada, the Louisville Institute, the Acadia Centre for Baptist and Anabaptist Studies, and First Baptist Church of Amherst, Nova Scotia. We thank Dr. Anna Robbins and Acadia Divinity College for contributing to the project in various ways and for cheering us on throughout our efforts—and Gordon Dickinson of Cloudfire Creative for our project logo, which has become this book's cover. We also appreciate the team at Wipf and Stock who have made the process of publishing this book so smooth: Matthew Wimer, George Callihan, Emily Callihan, Riley Bounds, and Ian Creeger. Many people have contributed to this book and our broader project, and for them we are truly grateful.

Introduction

In 2018, I (Melody) moved to Atlantic Canada and discovered a beautiful land near the sea, dotted with Baptist churches. "Are you pursuing ordination?" the interview committee from Acadia Divinity College asked me. Coming from a more restrictive environment for women in ministry, I was pleased to hear this question. I had indeed been feeling called to ordination, as my service among seminary students was a ministry. As I settled into my new position, I began to meet other women in Christian leadership and learn their stories.

I heard the same things repeatedly: "I was the first woman minister my church ever had." "God's call surprised me." "I received some sexist comments and wasn't sure what to do." These brief conversations left me curious, and I soon learned that around 125 women had been ordained by Atlantic Baptist churches, with the first ordination occurring in 1954. Some of the women ordained in earlier decades had already passed away, and others were in their senior years.

"Who will tell these women's stories?" I wondered. I realized that time was running out to capture this essential history. Someone needed to take action—and quickly!

I felt God calling me to take the lead on this important project, working alongside some talented research associates—including Joetta Fernando and Hannah Hunt, my co-editors. To date, our research team has interviewed more than one hundred women.[1]

1. These interviews are shared in an edited format on the *Called to Serve*

Most of these women were ordained by churches affiliated with the Canadian Baptists of Atlantic Canada (CBAC),[2] a denomination comprised of more than four hundred congregations across New Brunswick, Nova Scotia, Prince Edward Island, and Newfoundland. You'll meet fourteen of the women we interviewed in the pages that follow.

A STORY TO TELL

Josephine Kinley Moore was the trailblazer whose 1954 ordination at Prince William Baptist Church in New Brunswick proved a momentous first for Atlantic Baptists. Although several women had previously been licensed for ministry, the convention had not approved their ordination. In fact, in 1929 the convention's position was that "we do not favor the ordination of any woman at this time."[3] By 1954, however, two thirds of convention attendees voted in favour of Moore's ordination.[4] One pastor present on that day declared, "Ladies and gentlemen, do you realize that this is an historic moment in the life of our convention?"[5]

---

podcast, available at calledtoserve.ca and on Spotify and Apple Podcasts. At the project's end, complete interview transcripts will be donated to the Atlantic Baptist Archives at Acadia University in Wolfville, Nova Scotia.

2. In the past the CBAC has had different names, including the United Baptist Convention of the Atlantic Provinces and the Convention of Atlantic Baptist Churches. Throughout the book, we will refer to the group as "Atlantic Baptists" or the "CBAC." The CBAC is the largest Baptist group in Atlantic Canada and is one of four "convention" Baptist groups in Canada. The other three are the Canadian Baptists of Western Canada, the Canadian Baptists of Ontario and Quebec, and L'Union d'Églises Baptistes Francophones du Canada.

3. "Minutes of Convention," *The United Baptist Year Book of the Maritime Provinces of Canada, 1929* (Truro, NS: News, 1929), 17.

4. *The Year Book of the United Baptist Convention of the Maritime Provinces of Canada, 1954* (Saint John, NB: Barnes-Hopkins, 1954), 28–29; Hugh McNally, "The Convention of Atlantic Baptist Churches and the Ordination of Women," unpublished paper, revised edition, 2014, 4–5.

5. William Elgee, quoted in Hugh McNally, "Let's Keep on Ordaining Women," *Priscilla Papers* 11 (1997), https://www.cbeinternational.org/

While Moore would prove inspirational for many women who followed in her footsteps, this took time. Few other women were ordained in the years after Moore: only one in the 1960s and four in the 1970s. The first three of these women were in poor health or deceased by the time our project began, so the oral histories we recorded begin in 1976.

In the 1980s, the number of ordained women began to grow—as did opposition to women in ministry. By 1986, a vocal group within Atlantic Baptist life sought to end consideration of female candidates for ordination, leading to a vote on the convention floor the following year. However, this vote failed.[6] In the decades that followed, more than one hundred women were ordained by Atlantic Baptist churches. Starting in the 2010s, however, the number of women ordained declined slightly—a reminder that progress is fragile.[7]

Ordination within the Atlantic Baptist context involves a lengthy process. Candidates must be endorsed by their local church, complete interviews with the denomination's Board of Ministerial Standards, meet educational requirements, and fulfill extensive internship hours—all before they are interviewed by a formal examining council that votes on their fitness for ministry. Candidates who pass this examination are then ordained by their local churches in special worship services held for the occasion.

The women we interviewed faced both challenges and joys as pioneering women in ministry. Some experienced sexism from congregants, while others found new freedom in their roles. Women in churches associated with the African United Baptist

resource/lets-keep-ordaining-women/.

6. "Minutes of the One Hundred and Forty-First Atlantic United Baptist Convention," *1988 Year Book, United Baptist Convention of the Atlantic Provinces* (Saint John, NB: United Baptist Convention, 1988), 31, 33.

7. The total number of individuals ordained also declined—from 168 in the 1990s to 93 in the 2010s. However, an increasing *percentage* of individuals ordained in these years were women. In the 1990s, 20 percent of those ordained were women; in the 2000s, 34 percent; in the 2010s, 45 percent; and from 2020 to 2024, 28 percent. Thanks to Andrew Myers for his help with these statistics.

Association (AUBA) of the CBAC overcame additional obstacles to serve, sometimes encountering racial discrimination as well as opposition to the ordination of women within the AUBA.[8] A few ordained women chose not to participate in the project because of their negative experiences as women in ministry.

Throughout the wider CBAC, some churches and leaders continue to believe that only men should serve in pastoral ministry, but they are in a minority. In fact, at their 2023 convention, Atlantic Baptists appointed Rev. Renée MacVicar as the CBAC's executive minister, making her the first woman to serve in this role. We are grateful to Rev. MacVicar for writing the foreword to this book.

READING THIS BOOK

What can you expect as you read through the stories in these pages? You will hear from women of varied backgrounds, ages, family shapes, ministries, and passions. Each of these women's views are her own. No one person can speak for all women, but each story is a valuable and unique experience of calling, challenge, and service. There are as many ways to be a woman in ministry as there are women! Women serve as pastors, chaplains, missionaries, community leaders, and more. The fourteen women profiled in this book represent a sample of all those interviewed through Called to Serve.

As you read the stories in this book, look for threads of connection. What topics are mentioned consistently? How do the women's experiences intersect with each other? Where is God in their stories? How do they make sense of their callings and challenges? And what can their experiences tell us about ministry in the twentieth and twenty-first centuries?

Following each story are a few discussion questions. Feel free to use these for your own reflection, or for conversation with

8. The AUBA is a non-geographical association of the CBAC, encompassing churches with an African Nova Scotian heritage.

a group. We hope they will stir up thoughtful responses among readers.

Overall, we hope this book will help women and men—ministers and laypeople, in Canada and beyond—to better understand the experiences of women in ministry. We pray that the stories included here might inspire others to consider God's call on their own lives, and to persevere when they face difficulties in their lives and ministries. We also look forward to supporting female seminary students by donating all proceeds from this book to the Josephine Kinley Moore Bursary at Acadia Divinity College.

If you find the stories in this book compelling, there are dozens more posted on our website (calledtoserve.ca) and featured on the *Called to Serve* podcast (found on Spotify and Apple Podcasts). We encourage you to reach out to women in ministry in your own context and ask about their experiences. You never know when a story might just change your life!

1

Ida Armstrong-Whitehouse

Ida was ordained in 1976 at twenty-six years old. She has pastored both rural and urban churches in Nova Scotia, and served as a hospital chaplain for the Kings County Health and Rehabilitation Centre. In this chapter, Ida describes evolving attitudes towards women in ministry over her years of service. Her story demonstrates resilience in the face of struggles with cancer, infertility, and miscarriage, and church expectations around pregnancy and motherhood.

My name is Ida Armstrong-Whitehouse. I was born in 1950 in Middleton, Nova Scotia, the oldest of five girls.

My mom and dad were both Christians, and for them, faith was lived out in the home and not just at church. At the end of each day, before we children went to sleep, we'd kneel down with my dad by the side of the bed and pray for everybody we could think of: "God bless *you*, and God bless *you* . . ." It went on forever! My dad was often very tired, so sometimes he'd fall asleep and we just continued praying. Whenever we finished, we woke him up.

From a very early age I had a real experience of God's presence in my life, so when I was ten years old, I decided to make a commitment to Christ. That was considered too young at Kingston Baptist, but the minister advocated for me and I was able to be baptized—while wearing a crinoline!

Those years were probably the most intense season of learning in my life. The minister gave us all these Scripture passages and I just soaked everything in, like I never have since. Around that time, I also met Muriel Bent.[1] She had been a missionary nurse and midwife in India, and lived not that far from my family. Her ministry and how she related with people was an influence on me throughout my life.

When I was fifteen, I went to New Brunswick on my first mission tour. That was when I first realized not all Baptists thought alike. Up until that point, the churches I experienced all basically did the same sort of thing. But in New Brunswick when I was talking with people, I suggested that we play Crazy Eights, the card game, and they said, "Christians don't play cards." So then I said, "When I was driving up, I noticed that you have a drive-in theatre here. Wouldn't it be cool if we went to the drive-in together?" And they said, "Christians don't go to movies."

However, we were planning to invite the teens in the area to come see a film by the Moody Bible Institute. And there was a dance happening at the beach nearby. So I suggested, "Wouldn't it

1. Muriel Bent was featured on an episode of the *Atlantic Baptist Stories* podcast as well as the *Called to Serve* podcast. The episode is available at https://acadiadiv.ca/acbas/oral-history-project and on Spotify and Apple Podcasts.

be nice to take the teens to the beach and have a dance, and then we could all come back and see the movie?" And the people I was talking to went, "Christians don't *dance*!"

By that point I was wondering, "What do you guys *do*?" That's when I realized people have different interpretations of what being a Christian means.

A WOMAN OF PRAYER

I took my bachelor of arts at Acadia University from 1969 to 1972. I was trying to figure out what I was going to do and thought maybe I'd go into social work or teaching or speech pathology. I wasn't sure about my vocation yet, so I decided to go to the seminary for a year and get a better grounding in my faith. My parents were actually auditing courses at Acadia Divinity College (ADC) the entire time I was doing my undergrad, so the college was important in my family.

I didn't enroll in a specific program, so I was able to take any course I wanted, and I just had a ball with that! I enjoyed being with God and ministering in different ways, but I still had no sense of "calling." Then in the summer of '73, I was involved with an InterVarsity weekend camp where I was encouraged to look at my future in terms of discernment. It was an incredible experience, but I wondered, "What does this mean in terms of *calling*?" Because there's a difference between having a wonderful experience and being called.

So for the first and only time in my life, I decided that I was going to be like a four-year-old child, and I would ask God to give me a "fleece."[2] I laid the fleece out and prayed, "God, I don't want to tell anybody this, but if you are actually calling me into ministry, I need to know. I need to know because it's going to be a hard journey." I had to be convinced that ministry wasn't just something *I* wanted to do, but something God was calling me to.

2. See Judg 6:36–40.

So I said to God, "I've been at Acadia for a number of years now. I know how difficult it is to get an apartment, and it's the middle of August—most apartments are gone. So if you are calling me into ministry, then in the next two weeks I'd like you to present an opportunity where somebody asks me to share an apartment with them. I'm not telling anybody that I want one." Well, within ten days, I had three different people ask me.

The third person who asked happened to be the daughter of Reverend Josephine Moore, the first Baptist woman in the Atlantic provinces to be ordained in 1954. Rev. Moore was a woman of quietness and strength, a teacher by trade. Back then, if you were a teacher, you were also expected to look after some of the spiritual needs of the community. I asked her one time, "Would you see yourself as an evangelist?" And she said, "No, I see myself as a woman of prayer."

I thought that was lovely. That's really where the essence is. But I said, "Just by the way, though—have you, you know, helped people in terms of making a commitment to Christ?"

She goes, "Oh, yes."

I asked, "Did you baptize them?"

She said, "No, I get some of the men to do that."

So I asked, "About how many people would you say were baptized through your ministry?"

And she said, "Four hundred."

Oh my glory! Four hundred people made commitments to Christ through her ministry. And two of those people were Hugh McNally, who later became a missionary, and Ken Phillips, who became a leader in Baptist men's ministry. Both those men have talked about the impact Rev. Moore had on their life. So, meeting her was really helpful for me.

I started my second year at ADC and had some male students coming to me asking, "Ida, what are you doing here?" And I'd tell them, "I'm studying for the ministry."

They'd say, "Ida, you're a nice person. However, that's not biblical and you shouldn't be doing that. That's against God."

I knew that God had called me. I didn't understand it at all, but I was convinced, so I had to go with that.

They said, "You're making a big mistake."

STUDYING FOR THE MINISTRY

I was going out with a student who was one year behind me. He was in his first year, but he was a prize student; he was academically inclined.

We had a bit of a falling out, and by October of my second year, we had broken up. Gregg decided to leave ADC for a little while, and I decided to stay. I had a couple of professors come up to me and ask where Gregg was. I told them he'd decided to take some time off. Then they said, "Could we suggest that maybe you take courses at the Atlantic School of Theology in Halifax? Then possibly Gregg would come back." Well, nothing like not feeling wanted! That was really hurtful, and it made things very awkward.

I had a bit of difficulty in my third year. I was taking a hermeneutics course, and there were three of us in the course who were women, out of maybe twelve students. We were looking at what was going on with our grades. We didn't want to accuse anybody of anything, but we asked to look at the guys' papers and it seemed like there were some discrepancies with how the women were being marked.

One professor taught the first half of the course, and then there was someone else for the second half, so we decided to speak to the second professor about our marks. He agreed there was a problem. I asked what we could do about it and he said, "I'll give you higher marks in the second term. I don't want to rock the boat." So, we didn't rock the boat.

Gregg and I started dating again and then we got engaged. I was almost finished with my degree, but he still had another year of studies to get through. Back then, ADC didn't have any mentorship or internship as part of the MDiv[3] program—they initiated

3. Master of Divinity.

that aspect after I graduated. So Gregg spoke with the school's principal and asked if he would vouch for me so I could get a job in ministry. The principal said, "Well, if she was a missionary, I could." And Gregg said, "Well, she's not going to be a missionary right now. We're getting married this summer." Then the principal said, "Well, maybe I could get her a church for a year, and then when *you* graduate, you could take over!"

Gregg didn't think that was a good idea. He didn't even feel particularly called to pastoral ministry; he was interested in further studies and teaching. Anyway, in the end, the principal suggested a place I could supply preach, at a three-point charge nearby. It was just three little churches in Kempt Shore: Summerville, Bramber, and Cambridge—the biggest church probably had about fifty to sixty people, and the other two probably had twenty to thirty people each. And they were lovely. They called everybody up in those three communities—those who were Baptists and those who weren't—then called me back and said they wanted me. That was so affirming.

So it was 1975: I'd just gotten married, and we had no jobs and no money, but somehow it felt like in the midst of all this stress, God had already prepared a place for me. And I only needed one place.

NOTHING IS EVER WASTED

It was about a twenty-mile journey from one end of my pastoral charge to the other. Gregg was studying, and I had lots of time—no children yet—so I just had a ball. I went down the shore, visiting people and talking to them, and they were very gracious with me because there was so much I didn't know. But, I was a good listener.

At my request, I was informally mentored by an old Pentecostal minister—and between us, in the two and a half years I was there, I think we had forty funerals.

Going before the examining council was difficult. I knew going in that there would be people who couldn't vote for me because of their theological stance on women in ministry. So I was anxious as to whether there'd be enough people on council who agreed with it. But I thought back to Josephine Moore. When *she* went before the ordination council, one of the pastors stood up and said, "I'm against it." But then some missionaries got up and said, "Well, we aren't."

I was ordained in 1976 and asked Dr. Morris Lovesey, who was the professor of Old Testament studies at ADC, if he could be my ordination speaker. His sermon was on women in ministry—which wasn't at all what I was looking for. I was looking for something about being called by God, you know, whether you're a man or a woman. But I thought it was really sweet of him—he was wanting to take a stand and let me know that he affirmed me.

At the service, my husband sang, and my parents were there and laid hands on me with the deacons. I wore my wedding dress—which was a very plain white dress, so I dropped the train off and I thought, "Double duty!"

The following year, Gregg was asked to go to New Ross Baptist Church as their minister. I loved being with Summerville, Bramber, and Cambridge, but I thought, "He needs to have a turn, and God will provide some ministry opportunities for me." So we went, and then I was depressed. I was depressed for two months, crying most of the time—especially in church. I was really grieving the loss of my congregation and the ministry God had given me.

I had also become pregnant, but the pregnancy didn't work out; it became a molar pregnancy, which then resulted in cancer. So that was kind of a miserable thing to have happen.

But nothing is ever wasted with God, because at that point I was in my mid-twenties, yet looked about eighteen. I still looked like a young kid. Those experiences of depression and loss, however, provided a conduit whereby people trusted me at a deeper level, because they knew I had experienced pain. People were telling me about the losses they had in their own lives, and the cancer that had taken loved ones from them.

Did God give me the cancer? No, I don't believe he did. But I believe he brought good out of a bad situation. And so that deepened my ministry.

In 1978, the opportunity came up for me to be the chaplain at Kings County Health and Rehabilitation Centre[4] in the Waterville psychiatric hospital. Doing chemotherapy really helped me not to say stupid things as a chaplain! I knew what it was like to be mentally overwhelmed. That's when I realized how helpful symbols can be. I'd go to the hospital in regular clothes, then when it was time for worship, I'd put on a gown that Dr. Charlie Taylor[5] had given me. That was a cue to everybody that we were going into worship.

In addition to hospital chaplaincy, I worked at the Bible Society bookstore and ministered with a little Baptist church in Lapland, which is a place in the middle of nowhere. They were a great group of people. I was only there about two days a week, unless there were funerals or weddings or visitation that I needed to do. On Sundays, we'd have worship and then youth group, and I took the youth singing, skating—once to a synagogue in Halifax—just a variety of things. Again, we became a family. That's a model that works for me.

"WHAT DO YOU MEAN, YOU'RE PREGNANT?"

So I was quite happy with what I was doing. Then I got talking to a friend of mine, Byron Fenwick, who was the senior pastor at Kentville Baptist Church. He asked if I'd ever considered team ministry, and I said, "No, I have actually just given thanks to God that he has never called me to team ministry!"

In the previous year, I had counselled three people who were in team positions, and all of them were shafted by their senior pastors. That wasn't my idea of a good time. But Byron said, "It wouldn't be that way, working with me. Why don't you just come down and be interviewed?"

So my husband and I drove down to Kentville, and I cried all the way. My husband asked me why I was crying, and I said, "Because God might be calling me here, and I don't want to go!"

4. Now CORE Support Services.

5. Charlie Taylor was professor of clinical pastoral education at Acadia Divinity College.

After the interview, Byron asked me, "What's going on with you, Ida? That was the worst interview I've ever seen!" But once we got home, he called and told me that the church had voted unanimously to call me.

So that's where we went, in 1983. It was an adjustment for both Byron and me; our understandings of my job description were different, and in the beginning he wasn't keen on sharing some of the things that were important to both of us. But after about five years, we worked well together. There were about 350 people in that church. When I was interviewed, I told them I needed to do some preaching, some baptisms, and some marriages and funerals, so I had a very eclectic ministry. But that's what I felt most comfortable with. I'm a general practitioner, not a specialist.

At that point, Gregg and I were ten years without kids. I desperately wanted children, but it wasn't happening. I'd had cancer, and I'd had the chemo, and they said, "Oh, there's no problem." But yeah, there was a problem.

Anyhow, when things changed and poor Byron heard my news, he goes, "What do you mean, you're pregnant? I told the congregation you couldn't *get* pregnant!"

I went, "Why'd you say *that*?" And he goes, "Well, you had *cancer*! Oh, what are we going to do now?"

I said, "I'm going to continue to minister. I'm going to have a baby. The baby's going to be part of the congregation, and we're going to have a lovely time!"

I waddled up to the pulpit until the day before I had my first child. One of my deacons was also pregnant and waddling, so when we served communion, we had the table pushed a little further away from us!

AHEAD OF OUR TIME

I had both my children while I was at Kentville. At that point, there weren't good maternity benefits. After two months, I realized I would need to go back to the church half-time, as we didn't have enough money to live on.

After talking with the church a little bit, they asked if I would come back for thirty-five hours a week, and I said no. They said, "Well, you *were* working about seventy hours."

I was paid for forty hours, and I saw the additional hours I worked as a gift. That's when I realized I had created expectations because the church perceived those extra hours as part of my job. So that was a bit tricky.

My husband had planned on doing a Master of Library Science and actually began the program, but when our first baby arrived, he fell in love immediately. For someone who didn't really care if he had kids or not, it was automatic! He had been making straight A's and A pluses in his degree, but he decided he didn't want to do that anymore.

He asked me, "What are we doing, in terms of looking after Meaghan? How would you feel if I looked after her?" And I said, "Do you want to do that? I think that would be lovely!"

So Gregg looked after the kids, not working outside the home, and I was a pastor. I'm always curious to know how people saw this seeming role reversal—me being a mom, as well as a minister, and my husband staying home with the kids. I think we were a little bit ahead of our time.

Around 1987, Byron left Kentville Baptist. Most deacons were supportive of me staying on, but the chair of the deacons' board was not, and he was on the search committee for the new senior pastor. I met with him to hear what they were looking for, and I asked, "OK, but where do you see me fitting in?" And he said, "I don't."

That was painful. A congregation member told me, "Ida, that's not right." And I said, "I know it's not, but at this point, I've had a good ministry here. I'm not willing to fight it." So I resigned.

A few months later, I met Rev. Nelson Metcalfe at a wedding. He was a friend of Byron's, pastoring at Bedford Baptist. Byron had recommended me for Bedford, saying, "Ida would be great, but she's like a butterfly—she needs some freedom!" And that pretty well sums things up. That's who I am.

BEDFORD BAPTIST CHURCH

In 1988, with a two-year-old and a four-year-old, and a husband still at home with the kids, we moved to Bedford, Nova Scotia. I became associate pastor there and stayed for over twenty-seven years.

In terms of personality, Nelson Metcalfe was my direct opposite, so we very much complemented each other in our team ministry. My Myers-Briggs type is ENFP, and he was an ISTJ,[6] so that made it difficult because we didn't respond to things the same way. He didn't always know my plans, so I would try to give him a heads-up—but oftentimes I didn't know until I was starting something whether it would happen or not! However, because we both had the same deep call to ministry, it worked out well. Over time, things became more open-ended for me.

Being a woman in ministry at that time was enough of a novel experience that I had a lot more freedom than the men did. I could be myself more, because there weren't the same kinds of expectations placed on me. I think it was more acceptable for me to be creative or compassionate or show a softer side—whereas if I'd been a man, there were still a lot of stereotypes at that time.

I had three wishes in life; it sounds like a fairy tale. My wishes were to be a minister, to be married, and to be a mom. I feel that having children made my ministry more holistic and authentic, and being a mom was important to me.

At Bedford, I had this wonderful desk, and a chair that was *very* comfortable. My children had two little sleeping bags I kept underneath the desk. They loved their little hideaway and would sometimes fall asleep there. At one point during my time at Bedford, another church was asking me to consider pastoring them, and both my children went, "No, you can't go!" I asked why not, and they said, "Because this is our favourite chair!"

I figured if God was calling me somewhere else, perhaps we could find another chair.

6. For more on the Myers-Briggs Type Indicator, visit myersbriggs.com.

While at Bedford, I did a doctoral degree through Golden Gate Seminary[7] near San Francisco. The church was very supportive of me during those seven years and saw the degree as part of my wider ministry. They were supportive of all the things I was involved in, because I was also an RCMP chaplain for twenty years, and I served with Canadian Baptist Ministries on their board.

When I first arrived at Bedford Baptist, the church was probably around three hundred people, which was comparable to Kentville. There had been a great deal of debate among the deacons about calling me as an associate pastor. The big thing was, "Why can't she be a director of Christian education?" But that wasn't what I felt called to do. One of the deacons resigned over this, and it was very painful for him. But from his interpretation of Scripture, women were not appropriate for the role of pastor.

I was surprised, then, to see this man at my induction service.[8] He was there to show support—but not really. He hadn't realized that the question was going to be asked: "Would you please stand up if you support Rev. Armstrong-Whitehouse?" So he didn't stand up, and he was very embarrassed, and I was very embarrassed for him that he was in that position.

About three weeks later, we were attending a meeting and he needed a ride home, so I offered to drive him. We talked in the car, and he started crying. He said, "Ida, I didn't want to offend you. That wasn't my purpose. I just don't believe in women ministers." I started crying too, and I said, "I understand, and you'll be the very first person I'll tell if I feel God is no longer calling me to ministry." But I said, "You've got to be faithful to where you are, and I have to be faithful to where I am, and that's just the way it is."

Anyway, over the next twenty-seven-and-a-half years, I was able to baptize two of that man's three children and take part in all three of their weddings. His daughter once came to me and asked, "Ida, can I preach at the youth service this year?" And I went, "Ooh

7. Now Gateway Seminary.

8. An induction service is a formal ceremony that marks the beginning of a pastor's ministry at a church.

. . . have you talked to your father about it?" She said, "Yes, and he told me I must do what I feel called to do."

Isn't that something? It was interesting how people changed.

The principal at ADC who had struggled with me—I don't think he had any recollection of that later, at my induction service. His mind had been opened to the possibility of women in ministry. When he came, he said something to me like, "Oh, Ida, we're so proud of you at the divinity school for being a pastor in the church."

And I thought, glory be! If you wait long enough, maybe things will change.

Ida Armstrong-Whitehouse
Interviewed December 4, 2019

QUESTIONS FOR DISCUSSION AND REFLECTION

1. Ida shares her experience of growing up in a Christian family and being called to ministry at a young age. How did your family influence *your* faith experience? Was there anyone who advocated for you to use your gifts and talents?
2. Ida experienced loss and depression, describing them as conduits "whereby people trusted me at a deeper level, because they knew I had experienced pain." Likewise, she describes her struggle with cancer as something bad that God used to deepen her ministry, saying that "nothing is ever wasted with God." Has God ever used a difficult experience in your life for good?
3. Josephine Kinley Moore, the first woman ordained by the CBAC, served as a role model for Ida and inspired her to persevere. Do you have any role models? Have you ever shared your own story with others?

4. Attitudes towards women in ministry evolved throughout Ida's career. What changes in church culture have *you* observed over time? Do you agree that "if you wait long enough, maybe things will change"?

2

Joyce Hancock

Joyce was ordained in 1987 at First Baptist Dartmouth in Nova Scotia. She served as a missionary in Indonesia and Brazil, and today works for NorthWind Family Ministries in Thunder Bay, Ontario. In this chapter, Joyce describes her ministry to at-risk youth and how she helped develop a drug rehabilitation centre for young people in Brazil. She reflects on the advantages and challenges of serving as a single woman in ministry, and on the encouragement she received from other single female mentors.

My name is Joyce Hancock. I was born in 1955 in Thunder Bay, Ontario. My childhood church was Fort William Baptist Church, which is a member of the CBOQ.[1]

I felt the call at a really young age. I can't say exactly when, but I often talked about it. When people asked me what I'd do when I grew up, I'd say to everyone, "I'm going to be a missionary!" As soon as I could, I became involved in church. As a teenager, I taught the Bible in Sunday school and through the Inter-School Christian Fellowship; I really enjoyed the challenge of teaching and helping others to understand. My parents also made time for us to go to Dorian Bible Camp, which was a CSSM camp.[2] That was always a special week in my summer, because I lived on a farm and the rest of the time was farm chores. I became a camper and cabin leader and dishwasher and all those things you do as you grow up.

In those days, there were always missionary speakers at church and at camp. Sometimes the camp cabin leaders were missionaries who were home on furlough. So because many of my family members were teachers and I was interested in missions, I said I was going to be a missionary teacher. That was my focus right through high school. In 1974 I went to the Baptist Leadership Training School in Calgary, then back to Lakehead University in Thunder Bay for a bachelor of arts and bachelor of education.

I really didn't want to be in the classroom all my life, though. After substitute teaching for a little bit, I attended a recruiting weekend held by Canadian Baptist Ministries (CBM). They needed someone in Indonesia to teach the children of two missionary families, tutoring them through all the grades so they'd be able to carry on when they returned to Canada. Even though it was a world away, I said, "Oh yes, I'll do that!" My parents asked, "Could you possibly go any further?" And I said, "I don't think so—if I went any further, I'd be on my way back!"

So in 1979, as a brand new teacher, I probably took on a really big mouthful—but I was excited to get going and get into missions. I started working with those two families in Indonesia, as the only

1. Canadian Baptists of Ontario and Quebec.

2. Canadian Sunday School Mission, now One Hope Canada.

single person there. And actually, that was a really stretching experience for me. I found it lonely many times, and the only others who were anywhere near my age were the students. I had a really heavy teaching load because I was responsible for all the subjects for four students, and they were all in different grades. So I spent an awful lot of time lesson planning. I would not have wanted to do that forever, but I learned a lot during that time. I learned in some ways to speak up for myself, and to get over my shyness. In fact, when I came back to Canada, some people said, "Boy, we don't even know you!"

"WHY IS SHE NOT CALLED 'MINISTER'?"

I grew up assuming that when God calls you somewhere, he calls you forever to the same place, so I expected I would always be working in Indonesia. But that wasn't so. After four years my work was over, which took me a little while to accept. At first I wondered, "What did I do? What happened?" But now as I look back, I see that God had other plans.

I started at Acadia Divinity College in 1984, working towards a degree in Christian education. The professors were extremely encouraging, which was excellent, because there's no use offering degrees for women in ministry if they'll never be able to get a job. It was about the first time in my life that I felt somebody else was really pulling for me and I wasn't working on my own. I didn't sense any rejection from other students for being a woman—any comments made were more about my overseas experience, actually, because that was all I knew recently. I'd bring it up in class and they'd say, "Why do you always have to talk about Indonesia?" After graduating in 1985, I started at First Baptist Dartmouth as their director of Christian education. The lead pastor there at the time wasn't really anxious for me to be ordained right away. I felt it was not particularly important to him. I was called "director" there, not "minister," which I assumed was because I was a woman. When they hired a youth pastor, *he* was called "minister" and I continued to be called "director." I never had the fighting spirit to bring it up, but I think it came up in the congregation sometimes because I remember hearing things like, "Why is she not called 'minister'?"

And as a woman there, initially, I didn't receive as much pay. When budget time came around, some women in the congregation made a big deal about the fact that I was earning *much* less than the rest of the pastoral team. But what I heard from the lead pastor later was, "Oh, wow—you're getting a good increase this time! Aren't you lucky?"—as opposed to saying something more like, "The church has asked that you be put up to the level of the vision." It was the women who told me what they did, and I felt very loved and cared for in that church through instances like that.

In those years, there were motions coming forward in the Atlantic Baptist convention about whether they would continue to ordain women or not, but I didn't spend a lot of time thinking about it. It was easier for women to be ordained in Christian education, so I was kind of exempt from the contention. I was ordained in 1987 and my ordination certificate actually says on it: "Ordained in Christian Education."

The church in Dartmouth had about 250 to 300 people, and it was certainly a busy church! I took care of the Sunday school, filling in for classes that didn't have teachers, and was sometimes full time doing that. Sometimes I preached; occasionally, I married and buried, which I never thought I'd be doing. I did a fair bit of visiting people in the hospital and at home, and built up a single adults' group. We did quite big Vacation Bible Schools in the summers at that church, so summer was never a vacation time for me!

Then during the winter I worked with disadvantaged youth, and that work carries on today, which is gratifying. For a little while, some of them came to the youth group—they were a bit too rowdy, which the church didn't like very much—so it cooled off after a while, but I thought it was a tremendous outreach.

I really enjoyed my work in Dartmouth. I was extremely exhausted, but it was great, and I enjoyed the feeling of acceptance in the church. I'm still in contact with some of those people and every time I'm in the Maritimes, I go back.

Joyce Hancock

DEVELOPING A REHAB CENTRE IN BRAZIL

I left First Baptist in 1993. People at the church were very kind to say that the only reason they'd let me leave was because I was going overseas. During my time there, I'd done a few international youth mission tours with people from the area and taken some shorter trips to Bolivia, India, and Trinidad—so my heart was in missions, and they knew that. In '93, I was sent out by the Atlantic Baptist convention and went to Brazil long-term.

When I arrived, I was part of an experiment in language education. In Indonesia, I'd had to figure out how to learn the language on my own, but in Brazil they thought we could study the language and work at the same time. To learn, they sent us to a Catholic school in the capital city of Brasília, because that's where we'd be working. I was going to be working with street kids who didn't speak any English, so I really had to learn.

These were kids who really *did* live on the streets—we didn't just call them "street kids" like back in Dartmouth. In order to survive, these youth generally got involved with drugs of some kind. Alcohol, too, fairly often—but the real kicker was the drugs. In the area of Brasília where I was working at the time, it was mostly cocaine.

I went to be part of a team that was trying to reach out to these kids, but the Brazilian Baptist Convention didn't really know what they wanted us to do. They just said, "Do what you can to be a witness for them." So I spent a lot of time on the streets, trying to get to know the youth. Eventually I moved from working on the street to developing a rehab centre along with some Brazilian colleagues. And that was because the youth themselves said they needed two things: to get off the drugs, and to be able to learn some skills so that they could get "into" life, instead of always being on the edges of it.

Our program was fairly different from other programs in the area in that we worked with teenagers under eighteen years old. That requires a lot more rules with the government, so until we began our centre, there were only adult centres in the area. Now, unfortunately, it's become an adult centre as well and it runs in a much different format than we used. But at the time, my colleagues and I worked directly with young people. We fought for them in court, tried to get them back into school, and worked as hard as we could to get them into church.

We saw that if they could make a lifestyle change, they wouldn't go back to their old habits and old friends. And we found that they really could only do that by becoming Christians, because that would change their whole way of life. If they could really make that change, then they had all of life ahead of them. If they couldn't, and went back to what they were trying to leave behind, they generally lost their lives in it. We had a lot of success, and we had a lot of failure. That's how it goes with drug recuperation.

Those were hard years, but they were very good, too. I learned how God can really pull you through, and I felt that God was working in the lives of many young people. A number of them became Christians and will testify to the fact that without the ministry, there's no way they would've survived their experiences on the street. So, for me, it was a different kind of ministry. It was life and death.

A NEW WORK

The Brazilian Baptist Convention did not ordain women, and they did not appreciate the fact that I was ordained. I found that I was very often on the rejection side of things, and I was often out of the loop. I don't know if they even liked the work I was doing, because I was working with marginalized kids and troublemakers. It was work I had been asked to do, but I'm not sure a lot of them liked it. They probably figured it would be an older man and his wife who came down to do it, and it wasn't.

Because my work was very much in the community, I didn't insist on being called a minister or anything like that. But just knowing that I *was* a minister—a woman, and a single woman at that—it was easier for them to pretend I wasn't there than to deal with what they thought about women in ministry.

When I first went to Brazil, there were a few other CBM missionaries there, including a single person and a family. Soon, though, the single person was moved to Africa, and the family went to the Southern Brazil. So for a good number of years, I was alone in Brasília. There were times I wished for other missionaries around, but I was also quite happy to be with just my Brazilian friends and colleagues.

After about eleven years, CBM told me to pass the rehab work over to the Brazilian Baptist Convention. I knew that wasn't a smart thing to do, because at the time the convention wasn't very concerned with that kind of work. But I did it anyway, and they quickly made changes that I was sad to see.

I began a new work, based on a vision the Lord had planted in my mind a few years earlier. I wanted to do more prevention, to try and help kids find a lifestyle that would keep them off the streets. Along with Brazilian colleagues, we formed a work that carries on today; I'm still involved in it from a distance. We chose the community of Águas Lindas, because it was probably the most dangerous in the area and it was the community of most of the kids who came into rehab.

When we began, I rented a little place and said to the Lord, "If this is really your will, then you have to make the kids come. And we don't really have any money, so you just take care of that. You show us what to do."

Well, we had a tremendous response and outgrew the two little rooms that we were renting. We started helping women with coursework so they'd be able to get jobs, and generally tried to minister in the community, introducing youth to churches. The staff members we took on were from different churches in the town, so even though the organization was of Baptist background, we tried to minister to everybody and were seen as an interdenominational entity.

At crucial times, I seemed to have to go home on furlough and talk to CBM about what I was doing. I said that I would leave CBM, because this was the work God had called me to do. But the general director told me that, no, I wasn't going to leave—they'd do something to help me out and keep me there. So for ten years I worked with this ministry, helping it to grow up. I was in Brazil for around twenty-one years in all.

NORTHWIND FAMILY MINISTRIES

In the latter part of 2014, I came home to Ontario. My mom didn't know she needed care at that point, but my dad had passed away several years before. Through some of the things my mom was asking and complaining about, the Lord specifically told me, "You need to go home."

The first year back, my mom was still fairly independent. She wasn't quite sure where I got this idea that I should come and look after her, but it really didn't take long for her to understand that, yes, that's what God had in mind.

The Lord had been really gracious to me because, even before I returned to Canada, he put it in my mind that I'd be working with Indigenous people. After coming home, I saw a counselling course advertised online by a Christian organization that reaches out to Indigenous people. It was talking about teaching counselling skills to non-counsellors, like people who are in the church and want to be helpful. I thought that sounded interesting, and then after that course, I started hearing about NorthWind Family Ministries in Thunder Bay. That's where I now work.

They offer professional counselling, and do a family strengthening program that brings families from Northern communities, as well as from the city—mostly Indigenous families—to be able to work through some of their issues together in a counselling situation. I have several Bible studies going there now and can teach to my heart's content. I also have a prayer meeting with the older Indigenous women in their language, and started a worship evening. I found that as it's a phonetic language, I can sing along with them because I can do the phonetics, even though I don't technically know what I'm singing.

On Sunday evenings they offer a meal time and Bible study called the Gathering, which I take part in. Many of the people are low-income and really need extra help, so they need the meal as well as the teaching. They don't have to stay for the study, but we usually find at least half of them do. And since I started there and have been helping to build more things, people from the counselling aspect are invited to come, and others from the community come. It's become more of a church in content. The executive director, who is a wonderful Christian woman, has said a couple of times with amazement, "I have always said this is not a church. I'm beginning to think it is. It's a little different than the traditional church, but yes, it is." So I am just thrilled. God has given me the best of the best, in a sense.

SINGLE WOMEN ON THE FIELD

In Indonesia, they said they loved the work I did, but they'd prefer that I was married. That's not what I felt God had for me. I have nothing against being a wife, but I didn't feel that was what God wanted for me, specifically. I always wanted to be very involved in ministry, and I think being single opened up doors for me because I was freer to do things as they came up.

In Brazil as well, I think sometimes the church people expected to be working with a couple or with a married person. The Baptist church there grew out of Southern Baptist roots, and like the Brazilians, Southern Baptists did not ordain women—but they had an awful lot of single women on the field. So the Brazilians were not unfamiliar with single women working in some area of service. I think they saw me as a teacher—that was acceptable for a single woman in ministry, and they were used to that. However, if I had pushed the limits and wanted to be recognized as a pastor, I think there would have been a lot of trouble.

When I first went to Brazil and worked with the street kids, I spent a lot of time on the streets getting to know them and trying to help them trust me. I often went to the places where they hid, and I was often out at night. It was technically dangerous, but God always took care of that. I could not have done that as a married person—I don't think a husband would've allowed it.

And as a mother with responsibilities for children, I wouldn't have been able to be so free. I've thanked the Lord many times for that freedom; I've been very happy to be able to respond to whatever opportunity comes along.

Actually, I had many single female mentors. At First Baptist Dartmouth, there were a couple of single women older than me who were very involved in ministry and had a great effect on my life. I shared an apartment with one of them. She was alone at the time when I came and said, "If you're interested, I'd love to have a roommate." So we did that and shared expenses. She had a lot of expertise. She'd been a teacher for many years and was very involved in the church. Besides the wisdom she could share with me, and the way she did things and thought about things, I found that she was often the one who stood up for me. When I would come home and talk about something that happened—something I didn't like, that I was feeling awful about—occasionally she'd say to me, "That is not your fault. That's the fault of the other person who is responding to you." And to me, that was like turning a light on. Her perspective helped me—not to blame someone, but to understand what was going on. She recognized it right away. And so there were a number of single women who really helped me out.

Even as a child, I recall the lady who led the Dorian Bible Camp was a single female missionary, and she had quite an influence on my life. I think a lot of it was these women's dedication. Because they were single, they were able to respond to situations and live in certain conditions, because they were just taking care of themselves. I can look back with real delight in the friendships I had with them and the encouragement they gave me.

GOD HAS THE STRENGTH FOR ALL OF IT

Throughout the years, my path has changed. I hope that's been obvious. As I look back, I feel it has been of God's leading. Sometimes it's easier to see that when you're looking back than ahead. And I just praise the Lord for how he's taken the different situations in my life, good or bad, and worked them out and helped me to focus upon him.

I try to make sure that people in the ministry I'm in right now understand that God can do a lot for them. Partly because, with their history, they sometimes have difficulty believing that. There's a lot of different problems to work through. But I trust that God has me there for a reason. I think part of the reason is that I've worked through some similar difficulties, and I can testify that God has the strength for all of it.

God didn't say he was always going to lead me to easy things. But I did ask him to lead me into interesting things. When I was eighteen and probably not thinking about the number of years as they go by, I said, "Lord, I don't care how many years I live, I just want them to be *exciting*." And God has made that very, very true in my life.

Joyce Hancock
Interviewed January 30, 2020

QUESTIONS FOR DISCUSSION AND REFLECTION

1. Joyce describes receiving lower pay as a woman in ministry and not being given the official title of "minister." Do you think there is more equality in these areas today?
2. Although Joyce was aware of gender inequality, she says, "I never had the fighting spirit to bring it up." Do you resonate with her? Why or why not?
3. Joyce mentions that several single women encouraged and mentored her. How have you been mentored as a believer? In what ways could you support and encourage somebody else?
4. Joyce points to her singleness as an advantage that made ministry easier in a high-risk context. What are some of the advantages you have when it comes to serving your community?

3

Heather McGregor

Heather was ordained in 1994 at Port Williams United Baptist Church in Nova Scotia. She went on to serve as a nursing home chaplain in Wolfville, and as the coordinating chaplain for Valley Regional Hospital in Kentville. In this chapter, Heather describes the grueling experience she had going before the examining council on her road to ordination, and the contributions she made towards improving that experience for future ordination candidates.

MY NAME IS HEATHER MCGREGOR, and I was born in Ontario in 1941. While I was in ministry, I used the last name of Embree, but around 2010 I returned to my original name of McGregor.

I grew up in a time when everybody on the street went to church, and we were the only family who did *not*. At the age of nine, we moved from Ottawa to a Toronto suburb, and there was a church just half a block away. The minister called on my parents, so my father and I attended the service one Sunday morning. My father was disappointed there was no discussion of the sermon after the service, so he never returned. I, however, was allowed to go to Sunday school after that.

When I was about fifteen years old, a couple of girls from Sunday school invited me to attend a Billy Graham crusade, and that experience really got me questioning. I felt a real pull to go forward after the altar call one night, but my friends had already gone forward the night before and I was too shy to go alone. It was a huge conference.

When I got home, I told my father about this, and he kindly talked to me about mass emotionalism. He said it was probably a good thing I had not gone forward, as I really didn't know what I was doing—which was true!

During my university years, I met a young man in my summer work program who was a committed Christian. He talked about prayer being an important aspect of his life. I complained that I had *tried* prayer, but it never seemed to go beyond the ceiling. My friend was very understanding, and since we were both science students, he suggested an experiment. He said I should try praying every day for two weeks and see if I got through.

Well, I did as he suggested, and before the two weeks were up, I was astonished by the feeling that *somebody* was listening. That experience of being listened to changed my perception of God from an impersonal to a personal one.

I purchased a book that had an introduction to different parts of the New Testament, which I found very helpful. I was able to set what I was reading in context. I read straight through the New Testament in its entirety, in order to make sure there was nothing

I disagreed with. The more I read, the more I became drawn to the person of Jesus. I found myself wanting to live *my* life the way he'd lived his. So in my university residence room, without telling anyone, I quietly committed my life to Jesus.

After graduation, as a dietetic intern in Montréal, I participated in a small Bible study group. I started to feel a need for trained biblical teaching and developed the sense that one day I would study at a seminary. I had no thought of being eventually called into ministry; it simply began as a call to study.

A CALL TO STUDY

For the next several years, after I married, I took advantage of Bible studies in the area and raised my children. I led study groups, spoke at retreats, taught Sunday school to teenagers, and eventually taught the women's class at my church. I just had this constant hunger to increase my knowledge—until finally, I felt I was ready to go.

The Baptist seminary, Acadia Divinity College, was the closest seminary to where I lived. I wanted to study four subjects there as I felt this would give me a good enough basis to continue what I was doing with the women. So in 1982, I signed up for classes covering Old Testament, New Testament, systematic theology, and church history. However, once I began my classes, I found them very stimulating, and I went on to take more than four!

There were very few women students at the time I started, and the male students wouldn't really talk to the women. Out of all the men, there was only one who was friendly, and I appreciated his speaking to me and saying hello. But the majority ignored me; I just wasn't visible.

I had three growing children, so I took my courses one at a time. As I gradually accumulated credits, it dawned on me that I might actually graduate, which was never my idea at the beginning. So I asked myself what I'd like to do if I *did* graduate—and the answer came to me very quickly: I would like to be the chaplain at the regional hospital. I'd already been a hospital dietician and enjoyed that work, so I knew I'd find fulfilment in that setting.

In the summer of 1990, I entered chaplaincy at a local nursing home. My clinical professor suggested I apply for a position there, even though I had no experience with preaching or pastoral visitation. To my surprise, I was hired! But that meant I needed a church license, and *that* meant I had to appear before the Board of Ministerial Standards as a candidate for ministry.

Well, I still had my reservations about that. In fact, that question was the most emotionally demanding part of my journey. This was a time when many people still disagreed with women being in ministry, even though in 1987 the Atlantic Baptist convention had voted to accept it. I'd heard stories about the examining council, and they filled me with dread. As women, we knew there would always be votes against us. During some years, voters were counselled to abstain if the reason for their negative vote was gender, but in other years that recommendation didn't hold.

In order to be ordained, candidates had to complete a year of internship. This included having a formal mentor and an internship committee composed of people from your place of ministry. On my committee, I had residents from the nursing home, as well as the local minister. They examined every aspect of my ministry and reported on it, so the examining council could use these reports to inform their decision. I knew that my reports were very positive, so if anyone had their doubts about me, they could check my documentation and it should be OK.

Candidates also had to submit a statement of faith on various doctrines. And because I was so fearful about this whole process, I submitted my statement ahead of time to four professors—including the principal of the divinity college, who was the chief examiner. The principal said he might ask me more about the autonomy of the church, but otherwise he was satisfied with my statement.

Even though I was moving forward and had all this affirmation, I could not face the examining council unless I heard from God specifically. I needed to know it was *his* direction that I should proceed. I remember one professor told me, "You're like the person who stops on an island, and there's a boat there waiting to take you, but you say, 'No, I'm waiting for God!' Then there's an airplane ready to take you, but you say, 'No, thank you, I'm still waiting for God!'"

That really was a good description of what was happening to me.

A CHASM OF MISUNDERSTANDING

I prayed for months on end. While I was driving one evening, I could hear that my mind was saying something. When I listened, I heard the words of Jesus in the garden of Gethsemane: "Not my will, but thine, O Lord."[1] And I knew that just as Jesus dreaded his coming ordeal, yet he submitted, I was to do the same.

When the day came, I waited in the big lobby outside the lecture hall where the examinations were being held. Unfortunately, there was no privacy. People were passing to and fro, and they could come over and talk to you. That was difficult.

There was a gentleman being examined ahead of me, and my husband noticed he was sitting on a high stool and had his legs crossed in order to make a table for his papers. So my husband spoke to someone and said that, you know, I had a dress. He said, "My wife needs a table!" So they provided a "table," which was just a short footstool, so it was absolutely useless.

There was a man who led the candidates into the room, and when it was my turn, I felt a distinct contempt from him. I know I didn't imagine it because I later spoke with other women who had been through this process and each of them felt the same thing. It was something I just had to dismiss from my mind for that moment in order to continue.

I was ushered into the lecture hall and over to that high stool on the stage, which stood underneath a bright light. The entire hall was in darkness except for that light. It was so dark, in fact, that only people with really deep-set eyes were visible. And my stool faced away from the family and church members who were

1. Paraphrased. See Luke 22:42 (KJV).

there, so I couldn't get any encouragement from them. It was a very uncomfortable place to be.

The gentlemen on the platform were seated behind a table. These were various convention delegates, including the convention president who was conducting and monitoring the proceedings. I knew that he was *not* in favour of women in ministry. There was also the principal of the divinity college, Dr. Andrew McRae, who sat closest to me, and I was comforted by that. I had a reasonable relationship with him.

Dr. McRae began the examination, and he was very complimentary in his first statements, commending my doctrine of God. He also asked questions that surprised me. I was able to answer those, and then he turned to the council for their questions.

The next two questions I received were really good; I really appreciated them. One person asked how I would maintain connections—as I would be a chaplain, I could become like a Lone Ranger, so how did I maintain community? That question is so important. I explained that I certainly went to church every Sunday and gained nourishment from there; I also went to ministerial meetings in town, and knew a couple of women with clinical training like me. We were able to help each other with issues that perplexed us. That small group of women was actually part of my compliance with ethics requirements set by the Canadian Association for Pastoral Care and Practice[2]—pastoral caregivers had to engage in counselling, spiritual care, or a small peer group, so that they would never just launch out by themselves.

The other question I appreciated was about my prayer life.

But after that point, the questions became more antagonistic. One man wanted to know how I'd handle speaking to a person who had not yet made a commitment to Christ—and without waiting for my answer, he offered his own, saying, "You'd tell him he was going to hell!" I responded by saying that God is a God of love, and that I would *not* appeal to such a person in terms of hell. I knew my response likely solidified this man's vote against me.

2. Now the Canadian Association for Spiritual Care.

I was also asked to agree with a particular doctrine of Scripture that stated the biblical text was dictated directly by God. Because of the excellent biblical training I had received, I was not able to agree with this.

Another person accused me of seeking ordination because "you just want to lord it over us." Now, these are not questions. These are statements. And I felt really sad that there was such a chasm of misunderstanding between us.

"THE COUNCIL PREFERRED A MURDERER"

As the questions at my examination went on and on, I began to hear in my mind that verse from Ps 22: "The bulls of Bashan surround me." I became extremely tired and thirsty, and I couldn't see how the men's questions were really examining either my theology or my ministry. It was distressing.

When they finally said it was over and I left that hall, I knew I had stayed true to my beliefs. I hadn't perjured myself in any way.

I waited again in that big lobby room, with people walking to and fro. As members of the council and other observers left the examining room, no one even looked in my direction. Finally, my area minister[3] gave me the news that I had *not* received sufficient votes to be ordained. However, he said there was a lot of upset around this decision. He told me they had scheduled a reconsideration for nine o'clock that evening which I needed to attend, so I waited around all day to hear my final result.

Over lunch, the president of Atlantic Baptist College[4] asked me if I could change my gender before the evening meeting. His comments solidified to me what the issue was. The only other woman who appeared before the council that year was also denied, while the eight male candidates all received sufficient votes to move forward.

3. An area minister supported churches and ministers in one part of Atlantic Canada.

4. Now Crandall University.

Later that evening, after waiting for hours outside the meeting room door, I was called back in. There, it was declared there'd been a miscarriage of justice, and I had now been accepted and was welcome. One person told me later that the "miscarriage of justice" had to do with my statement of faith and that of a male candidate's. Apparently, except for two areas, our statements were practically identical, and while that candidate had received sufficient votes, I had not.

I was very puzzled by this explanation, as I had not given my statement of faith to anyone but my professors. A few days later, I voiced my confusion to one of them and learned the answer.

One of the male candidates had served time in prison for murder years before. He'd since experienced conversion to Christ and felt called to the ministry. But when he showed our professor his statement of faith, it was found lacking, so the professor gave him several other statements to review, removing any identifying markers. One of those was mine; the candidate had obviously identified with it, explaining why ours were so similar.

After explaining the situation, my professor addressed me—and I'll never forget his words. He said, "Your own work has saved you, Heather. The council preferred a murderer to a woman."

SERVANT, PROPHET, PRIEST, AND SHEPHERD

I was ordained at Port Williams United Baptist Church[5] in November of 1994, about three months after my examination. At the service, my minister began to describe my encounter with the examining council as "grueling"—then he stopped himself and went on with the planned ordination.

The nursing home I worked at made a real effort to bring as many residents as possible who would benefit from that kind of service. I thought it was important to use symbols that spoke to the work I did as a chaplain. I chose the basin and towel, symbolizing

5. Some Atlantic Baptist churches include "United" in their name because the convention was created from a union of two different Baptist groups. These churches are not affiliated with the United Church of Canada.

the service of Christ, and I had one of the residents from my internship committee present that to me. I felt really good about that.

I had another person present me with a Bible, which represented the prophetic aspect of working as a minister or a chaplain. Then someone presented a gown, which alluded to Israel's high priest Aaron, representing a minister's priestly function: presenting God with the concerns of the people, and presenting people with the concerns of God.

Finally, someone presented me with a shepherd's crook, to symbolize my being an "undershepherd" of the Good Shepherd, Jesus.

I very much enjoyed my work at the nursing home: visiting residents, supervising students, and leading worship services. I provided funeral services at the request of some patients' families, and I even officiated weddings for several of the staff. It was very enjoyable work, though it did not pay very much.

Shortly after going before the examining council, I was asked to meet with my minister and the incoming CBAC president to provide suggestions for improving examinations in the future. My first comment to these gentlemen had to do with the abysmal pastoral care of the candidates. They were somewhat surprised by this, as though nobody had ever thought about the candidates needing pastoral care.

I told them the candidates would be better served by having a quiet, private room, where they could wait their turn and hear their results afterwards. Ideally, there should be a compassionate minister assigned to them, so they could spend some time collecting their thoughts beforehand and process their experience.

I suggested that the examination hall should be well lit; you should be able to see everybody in attendance. Instead of sitting on that uncomfortable high stool, candidates should have a chair with a back and a table for holding their papers. And there should be water available—I remembered just how thirsty I'd felt.

I suggested there be a limit on the number of questions one person could ask, because at my examination there was a group of five or six council members who kept rotating their questions.

I believed that if a candidate was denied, a documented reason should be provided, because they certainly didn't document any reasons about me.

Finally, I said there needed to be greater gender equality on the council. The council was composed of a member from every association in Atlantic Canada, and at my examination they were all men. I thought there should be an effort made to get more women, because a woman needs another woman in the room. Even back when I first went before the Board of Ministerial Standards, I saw one woman in that room and immediately thought, "Oh, *good*—there's a woman." But then that meeting started and I realized she was the secretary, taking everything down but not engaging in the conversation. So there were sixteen men interviewing me, and that's a powerful experience for any woman to have when you're going before them as a candidate.

I am glad to be able to report that at least three quarters of my suggestions were put into practice. Over the next few years, I attended some of those examinations and I truly was comforted to see that the examining council had become much more humane.

A PART OF THE TEAM

In 1997, the position of coordinating chaplain for Valley Regional Hospital in Kentville, Nova Scotia, was advertised. The community had raised funds for this position because they wanted a chaplain who wasn't financially dependent on the government, so the role was near and dear to their hearts. I served in that role from 1998 until 2010.

At the hospital, of course, I was working with people from all kinds of denominations, not just Baptists. And so it was an altogether different atmosphere than I had experienced at Council. Very occasionally, I would enter a room and get an icy cold feeling from a patient, but I would just greet them and move on, knowing not to push anything. For the most part, people would tell me, "I'm so glad you got this job!"

I carried a pager at all times, and over the years I was called to crises in all departments of the hospital. The most difficult calls for me were pregnancy, infant loss, and car accidents where children were involved. I attended ICU rounds and weekly rounds on the medical and surgical floors, and anybody who was in the hospital for more than nine days was also on my possible list of visits.

Generally, when entering an institution, it takes a long period of time to earn acceptance, and the discipline of chaplaincy is not familiar to many. After a year and a half at the hospital, there was an emergency call one night. I could hear the nurses who were attending to the patients whispering, "*She's here . . . She's here . . . She's here . . .*"

I realized they were looking for me, and that I was being accepted. I began to feel like I was part of the team.

My chapel volunteers told me that patients were always saying, "We're too sick to get in a wheelchair and go down to the chapel, but we'd really like to watch the service. Why can't this be on the television?" So I got them to write a letter, and I signed it and took it to my supervisor. It wasn't long before we were able to get the in-house channel available so we could televise the chapel services through the hospital.

When volunteers went around to the patients, I had them ask if anyone wanted their name mentioned in prayer during the service. Often, there were up to forty names that we shared. There were times when I had the opportunity to see some of those people, maybe a day or two later, and they'd say, "I heard my name last night!" You could see that was supportive to them, which gave me a lot of joy as well.

I also did some advocacy work for the hospital clergy. The hospital paved its parking lot and so they started charging everybody for parking—of course, even the staff is charged. I went to the administration and told them I was concerned that clergy weren't able to park free of charge. I said, "These people come as volunteers, yet they really are part of the healing team at the hospital." And the hospital considered it and agreed.

I planned annual educational visits for clergy and lay pastoral visitors to try and upgrade their understanding of the illnesses people were facing. We had a cardiologist come and talk, and people who'd had cardiology problems came and shared their story. We did the same thing for cancer, and schizophrenia, and stroke. I believed it was part of the hospital's work to educate, so that people could get the best care possible.

I was also aware that many clergy are on their own. I mean, there are a wide variety of denominations, and many churches don't know that they should give their clergy a break to go on a retreat. So we decided to hold a retreat every year, thinking perhaps local churches would give permission for their clergy to attend if the hospital organized it. It gave ministers a day to come and hear speakers and reflect on their own ministry.

Those were some of the things I did in my ministry that I felt really good about.

THE WORK I WAS MADE FOR

The year that I went before the examining council, there were many people who came up to me afterwards. I remember one man said, "I feel so embarrassed by the convention. This is just not right."

But I also had *women* who came and didn't understand why I would be doing this at all. And I think that, over the years, things have certainly changed. More people accept women in ministry. Churches want more than one minister now; they're looking to have diversity. And diversity could mean a woman, or a Black person, or an Indigenous person.

So I think there's more openness, and we are progressing, but there's certainly still the other side of the coin, too. Issues come up and we have to deal with them. We're always going to be struggling with the perception that women should not be in ministry, and it is a barrier. My gratitude goes out to Acadia Divinity College for their affirmation and support at a time when it was very challenging for women called to serve. Ministry became work that I truly loved, and that I felt I was made for.

Heather McGregor
Interviewed June 10, 2022

QUESTIONS FOR DISCUSSION AND REFLECTION

1. What would be challenging about serving in a hospital or nursing home setting? What would be rewarding? Have you ever considered being involved in that type of ministry?
2. Heather's suggestions resulted in changes to the examining council process. How do you think those changes have improved the experience for other ordination candidates?
3. What challenges have you faced because of your gender, ethnicity, or identity? Has your faith helped you face those challenges?
4. Have you ever encountered a situation in which broader, systemic change was needed? How did you respond?

4

Barbara Putnam

Barbara was ordained in 1996 in Nova Scotia. After witnessing the aftermath of a significant passenger flight accident, she entered a career in military chaplaincy. In 2016, she became the first woman to attain the rank of colonel in the Royal Canadian Chaplain Service. In this chapter, Barbara reflects on the highlights and challenges of her career, including how she responded to 9/11, the dynamics of team ministry in multi-faith environments, and her recent work with Operation HONOUR, in which she helped address issues of sexual misconduct in the military through a process of restorative engagement.

My name is Barbara Putnam. I was born in Saint John, New Brunswick, in 1966.

My family and I were charter members of Nerepis United Baptist Church, which was a new church plant in my community. I was involved in church life from an early age, teaching Sunday school and leading the youth group and singing in the choir. I was even church secretary for a while, and I did camp ministry and was president of Atlantic Baptist Youth.

While completing my first undergraduate degree at the University of New Brunswick, I had job prospects to work as a computer programmer. I loved working with computers and loved technology—I still do! But all of a sudden, moving in that direction as a career was not what I wanted anymore. I knew it wasn't the right thing.

Instead, what came to mind as the right thing was going to seminary and exploring a call to ministry. It was eye-opening for me to realize that what I'd been doing all along was what I was meant to be doing for the rest of my life. I remember being almost shy to tell my best friend about it. She just looked at me after I told her and said, "I've known all along you would do this!" I was like, "Well, why didn't you tell *me*? It would have been nice to know all along too!"

I'm very thankful for the positive influences that were around me during that period of time. Of course, my church had known me for my entire life and was incredibly supportive. My parents were also supportive, although wondering what I was getting myself into, because they both understood what ministry life was like. And Brad, whom I married in 1995, couldn't be more supportive of me, and of women in general doing anything they want to do.

Growing up in New Brunswick, I did not see women in ordained ministerial roles. There were obviously lots of fabulous women in Christian education with youth and children—and in fact, when I applied to go to seminary, I initially enrolled in the Master of Religious Education program, not in an ordination track. However, after my first semester, I switched to the Master of Divinity degree program. There were several women studying at

Acadia Divinity College (ADC) at that time, and they became my colleagues and friends. We shared casual conversation, times of prayer and worship together, and chats in the hallway discussing what we were about to do.

My background was in rural churches, so I asked to have my supervised field education in a city church. I was placed at First Baptist Church Halifax, where I learned an incredible amount about liturgy, and about the importance of music and its historical aspects. That placement gave me a different view of church operations—not that the church is run like a business, but there are principles about how to run a church that keep it healthy, keep it safe, keep it diverse, and keep it afloat in some cases. I have always tried to incorporate what I learned from them into my ministry practices.

SUPPORT FROM AN UNEXPECTED CORNER

I am part of a clergy couple, so Brad and I graduated and were ordained together. We went before the examining council in 1995, and would've both passed unanimously, except there was one individual who was well known for being dead set against women in ministry. No matter what I said, he was going to vote against me, and so he voted against my husband too. Despite that, our ordination ceremony was a joyful time. The speaker was one of our former professors, and we chose the grandest hymns, because the church we were ordained in had a lovely pipe organ and the organist loved to play majestic pieces. It was a wonderful beginning to our ministry lives.

We pastored in Lunenburg County on the South Shore of Nova Scotia until 1998. Then in 1999 we moved to New Brunswick, where I was called to be interim Associate Pastor at Sussex United Baptist Church. They were originally wanting to call a youth pastor, but when I interviewed, we agreed that my leadership skills could be used more effectively as an associate. I thoroughly enjoyed preaching and leading services at Sussex, and the youth were fantastic. I was fully integrated into the ministry there.

One of my best memories from that pastorate was working with the deacons' board. They were your traditional senior male leaders, and were so positive about me being there. They supported me and pushed me to do as much as possible in that church, and I never forgot the support I received from that unexpected corner. You just never know, as a woman, whether support will be given or withheld. But they did a beautiful job, those Christian men, of saying, "We are with you, we support you, we want this, and we want this for you."

In the summer of 2000, that church actually called me to stay in a full-time role. But I had begun the long process of applying to military chaplaincy. God's humour showed up, because the day after Sussex called me, I finally heard I had a job offer from the military—and basic training was going to start in three weeks! I truly felt awful having to go back to the church and say, "You know, we thought my pastoral role was going to be permanent, because we thought this military thing wasn't going to work out. But lo and behold, here it is, and it is my calling. I need to go."

Once again, the church in Sussex was incredibly gracious. And I know they've had fantastic pastors since then and didn't miss me for a minute!

CALLED TO MILITARY CHAPLAINCY

My call to military chaplaincy came in a very specific way. While we were pastoring on the South Shore in Lunenberg County, the Swissair Flight 111 plane crash happened. From where our house was, we heard the crash, we felt the crash, and we responded to the crash as pastors. In the days that followed, local clergy began supporting the community and its first responders, including the members of the Canadian Armed Forces (CAF) who were called in to support cleanup efforts.

The military was in our town for weeks, working along the shoreline. I started to wonder how they could do that and what supports they had, because the kind of work they were doing was clearly going to have mental health and spiritual repercussions.

How would they be resilient in the face of that much trauma and tragedy? I didn't know the answer, but I was very curious.

Several months later, Brad and I were on vacation, and we just happened to meet two military nurses from the Halifax area. They recruited me right there on the beach, saying, "We need people like you in the military!" So when we returned home, as I'd promised those nurses, I went to my local recruiting centre. Unfortunately, this centre had never recruited a chaplain before. They gave me a one-page document that explained how chaplains take care of people and do church services, and I was like, "Thanks; I'd figured that much out!" But they promised to call with more information.

I walked back to the car where Brad was waiting, and he asked me how it went. I said, "I'll never hear from them again!" However, the next morning, the phone rang. It was Dr. Andrew Irvine, who was the director of the Doctor of Ministry program at ADC. He said, "I hear you want to join the military! I'm the chair of the selection committee for Canadian military chaplains." I'd actually been Dr. Irvine's teaching assistant and had no idea that he was on that committee or doing that work.

So it wasn't the military lifestyle that attracted me—not the uniform or moving around the country. It was just a sense that there are people doing work on behalf of Canadians who need spiritual support, and I believed I had what it takes to do that.

When I received the military's job offer during my time in Sussex, I had three weeks to prepare. The senior chaplain who called me said, "We're posting you to Petawawa." And I responded, "OK—where or what is Petawawa?" I think he must have rolled his eyes, like, "What does this woman want with us? She doesn't know anything." And that was true!

So in the fall of 2000, I showed up for basic training in Ontario, at Canadian Forces Base (CFB) Borden. I'd never even taken my uniform out of its cellophane bag. You're supposed to be green when you're in the army; well, I was *really* green. Almost a quarter of a century later, reflecting on my military career as it winds down, I know I'd absolutely do it all again in a heartbeat. Despite my trepidations at the beginning about what it would look like and how basic training would go—well, out of twenty-five years, those were just thirteen weeks. A very small part of my journey was the part that I feared most.

AFGHANISTAN AFTER 9/11

God gave me courage every step of the way. And courage was needed. As a newly minted captain, I became a unit chaplain for a service battalion and field hospital in Petawawa, Ontario. Just as I was settling in and learning how to bring my pastoral skills to that new environment, everything changed. After the Twin Towers fell on 9/11, we were deployed to Kabul, Afghanistan, and I was there for a little over six months in 2003 as part of Operation ATHENA. Our team of four chaplains provided religious support, ethical advice, and ministry of presence to a multinational brigade. That experience was life-changing.

I was in a bunker one night when there was a threat of a rocket attack. We were handing out jujubes and trying to make coffee—just trying to keep everybody in good spirits for hours while we waited for the "all clear." And the thought just occurred to me, "What's a little girl from Westfield, New Brunswick, doing in a place like this?" And I thought, "*Lucky me*." I knew I was in the right place at the right time.

For years, Canadian soldiers, sailors, and air personnel were known as peacekeepers. In fact, based on a recent survey, that is still what most of the Canadian public believes we do. The impact of 9/11 was that for the first time in many years, we were in a combat role. We lost 159 soldiers and seven civilians during the ten years the CAF was in Afghanistan. So we needed to do a lot more work in mental and spiritual health. Because there's nothing worse on operations than a death; it impacts everyone.

All of this loss, grief, and trauma reoriented our pastoral care towards a focus on resiliency and spiritual health. While the military's Health Services continued developing mental health resources, our chaplaincy work focused on spiritual resiliency—and on resiliency in general. We had to prepare people to face the possibility that people would die on your tour. Whether you looked left or right, you didn't know if it was your buddy or your friend or *you* that wasn't going to make it home.

We did a lot more next-of-kin notifications during that period. The chaplain and the commander would get in a car with a team and go notify a person's parents or spouse that the worst possible thing had happened. And that's not easy. Whether it was a death, or an accident, or some other reason we had to knock on a door, we worked really hard on being both caring and professional—learning to understand trauma better, so we could be compassionate and trauma-informed.

Then of course, we were involved in planning funerals for the families and the unit and the bases to get closure—and for Canada to understand the sacrifice. We've all seen the pictures of people standing on the bridges over Ontario's Highway of Heroes, the route from the mortuary to the cemeteries where officers are laid to rest.

We put a lot of effort into better understanding the impacts of grief, trauma, and sacrifice. For example, we've worked to improve the transition process for veterans returning home, trying to provide them with a soft landing spot and reduce the stigma around PTSD. We want veterans to know that although some days are bad—maybe all days are bad—you can get through them. Someone is there to help who truly cares.

A COLONEL IN THE ROYAL CANADIAN CHAPLAIN SERVICE

When I came home from Afghanistan, I was posted to a training base at CFB Gagetown, New Brunswick. That's the only time I was ever posted back "home," as I'd call it. I was the chapel life coordinator there, and also had my first taste of working inside an Air Force unit, which I loved. Brad and I bought our first home during that time, and we lived close to family and friends, so there were lots of firsts there and a lot of good times.

During that posting, I completed a full year of language training. Everyone in the military is supposed to have at least a passing ability to speak a second language, and over your military career, your proficiency is supposed to increase. So I was very fortunate to be put on a year-long course to learn French, which would have made my grade ten French teacher fall over in disbelief! After completing that course in 2007, I was promoted to the rank of major and posted to CFB Borden in Ontario, to the Canadian Forces Chaplain School and Centre.

At the Chaplain School, my work was completely different. I led a team that worked on improving our chaplaincy curriculum, adding technology and remote learning to all our courses. It was the first complete restructuring of curriculum in the history of the school, and it was a privilege to be trusted with the future learning of our chaplains.

Then I was dragged away from my desk to go to the Joint Command and Staff Program in Toronto at the Canadian Forces College. That was a leadership training course, and I met incredibly gifted individuals there. Probably around 18 to 20 percent of people in our course were women, and they were senior-ranking, because everybody was at least a major or a lieutenant colonel. So we had quite a bond together, living in dorm rooms and going to classes every day. It was like a redo of university life, in a way, and that's an invaluable network I still have today.

In 2011, I was posted to the National Defence Headquarters in Ottawa to be the chaplain general's aide-de-camp and staff officer. I leaned heavily on my colleagues from the leadership training program, because working in Ottawa is very different from life on a base. I supported the chaplain general with all his travel and activities and speaking engagements, and I learned all about late hours and travel myself. It was a tough year, but a rewarding one. At the end of it, I was promoted to the rank of lieutenant colonel, and in 2013 I became the deputy director of chaplain services. I was involved with recruiting new chaplains and bringing them into the fold.

Something truly significant happened the following year, in 2014, when I became one of three female chaplains selected to be command chaplains for the CAF—meaning I became the senior chaplain for the entire Royal Canadian Air Force. A United Church chaplain was selected for the Canadian Army, and an Anglican chaplain was selected for the Navy. So for the first and only time, all three senior lieutenant colonel positions were held by women.

Finally, in 2016, I was promoted to the rank of colonel. I am the first woman to attain that rank in the history of the Royal Canadian Chaplain Service. As Colonel, I was the director of chaplain operations, the chaplaincy chief of staff, and the director of chaplain services. It's been quite a journey from being a brand-new green captain who didn't even know where the military base was, to becoming a decorated female colonel.[1] It's been a great twenty-four years.

WE CAN'T DO IT ALONE

I will always identify as Baptist because I'm very proud of where I come from. When I first joined the military, there were only 150 chaplains, and only eight of them were Baptist. I was told, "As soon as a Baptist chaplain retires, we can bring you in, because we can't have any more than eight." Now there's over fifty of us, from ten unique Baptist denominations! We've worked really hard to share our ministry and what we do, raising awareness and actively recruiting people to bring them in.

Chaplains need to maintain a relationship with their sending denomination. In practice, though, that's quite difficult. I think chaplains of any faith struggle to maintain connection with where they came from, but it's especially difficult in the Baptist world. The Baptist church in one town is not the same as the Baptist church in the next town, or even on the next street over. You can feel very disconnected from your church or faith group, but you *need* to

1. Barbara is a recipient of the General Campaign Star, the Queen's Diamond Jubilee Medal, and the Canadian Forces Decoration. In 2019, she was named one of the Top Ten Women in Defence by *Esprit de Corps* magazine.

keep those connections. You have to work hard to stay grounded in your own tradition, because that is why you're here. You are sent; you're not let go. And one day you will return to the fold.

We've worked with all our Baptist conventions across the country to help them understand the work we do, because the more they understand, the more they reach out and include us in things like spiritual direction programs and pastoral retreats. We've been intentional about telling them, "You sent us to do this ministry, and we want to be accountable to you by sharing the stories of what we're doing."

Chaplains see a lot of stuff, and we have to grow up really fast in the military. So it's vital that we keep strong, keep fit, and remain resilient. Like many chaplains, I have a coach and spiritual director, and it's important we check in with each other. I've mentioned my spouse Brad a couple of times, and I couldn't imagine this journey without him. I think every minister would say they need people to support them, because we really can't do it alone. I know some people think they can, but eventually they learn it's better when you have others to rely on.

VOCATIO AD SERVITIUM: A CALL TO SERVE

The motto for the Royal Canadian Chaplain Service is "*vocatio ad servitium*," which is Latin for "a call to serve." We're getting more and more young chaplains interested in this specialized ministry. But it has to be a calling. Sometimes interested people come to our information sessions and I've talked them right out of joining, simply because military chaplaincy is a completely different style of doing ministry than what they're used to. Others realize they *are* well suited, even if they initially dismissed the idea.

When you're a solo pastor in a church, you're responsible all the time for everybody. My hat goes off to those in pastoral ministry—it's not easy, and you're often alone. That's a totally different ministry style than working on a multi-faith team, where you can just hand over the phone and know nobody is going to call while you're on leave. Chaplains work in teams almost exclusively. My calling has been to live out life's experiences in the same way my colleagues are doing: I run through the muck, I put a fifty-pound pack on my back and go for a walk, I wear the uniform, I abide by all the policies everyone else does. But I am different because I am the chaplain. I represent the spiritual.

We have chapels and chapel groups—they're called "faith centres" now, because they're open to all faiths. So we work not only ecumenically, but in a multi-faith environment with other religions. When you sit around the table and decide who's getting posted where, you consider both the needs of the chaplain and the community they serve. We need to know: do we have enough Protestants in a certain location? Do we have someone who can do an infant baptism? Do we have enough French or English chaplains? We also respond to requests for imams, rabbis, or humanist chaplains.

We are continually evolving in our understanding of how to cooperate in this ministry together, knowing that we don't necessarily share all the same beliefs or practices, but are seeking to build a deep respect for the faith traditions of others. We can work together and have fun together, and we can do the main thing, which is to provide religious and pastoral support to anybody who comes through our door. Sometimes I can provide that support, and sometimes I need to refer to somebody else. Like if someone comes in looking for financial aid, I might be able to help, but they also might need to be referred to a financial expert. As chaplains, we do that triage because we're the frontline resource for everyone. And we're confidential. Everyone knows they can come to the Padre—they can talk to us about anything and it stays with us. The trust they afford us is so important for what we do.

I'm not sure what the public sees when they look at military chaplains. They see a chaplain when they go to a cenotaph on Remembrance Day, but I don't know if they fully comprehend our work. We don't just lead services—we spend our days looking for ways to improve quality of life. We have a "ministry of presence," day in and day out. I've experienced the joys of doing weddings and baptisms, but I've also met people on the battlefield in their worst moments. I've met families in their worst moments. When people are injured, physically or psychologically, it's our obligation and our privilege to care. Being present to people is what we do.

Chaplains also have opportunities to influence at the highest levels and to give ethical advice to the most senior leadership. Still, the majority of chaplains are at the initial rank of captain or lieutenant, and they're on the ground with their troops all the time. So there's a variety of ways to serve, but it all starts with the part we love most, which is working with the soldiers, sailors, air personnel, and their families. It is a ministry like no other.

We have military families in many of our communities, and I encourage local churches to be aware of their unique needs. There are also kids in Cadets, and Cadet camp chaplains are needed. Reserve unit chaplains are needed for part-time ministry as well. So there are many ways indeed to be called to serve!

OPERATION HONOUR

The military is a federal government institution that affords all the protections that come with a government job. So, equality of pay and the ability to move up in rank are all there. Those policies apply to everyone, regardless of gender, and women are in every trade. But let's be honest: the military has been in crisis in recent years. Damaging sexual misconduct scandals have come to light, and several Supreme Court justices have recognized that we must change our culture.

In 2015, the trajectory of my work changed. I became involved with Operation HONOUR, a several-years-long effort to eliminate sexual misconduct, harassment, and discrimination from the Canadian Armed Forces. I focused all my efforts on attending to the sexual misconduct crisis that gripped the CAF, which included a final settlement agreement for those who had experienced sexual assault, harassment, or discrimination. Too many men and women—myself included—were harmed in some way over the course of our service to Canada.

In 2022, I began working full-time in the area of restorative engagement, bringing my pastoral skills to the task of listening, caring, and bringing comfort to those who have been harmed. The restorative engagement process was developed because of the lawsuits brought forward by former members of the Canadian Forces. We wanted to use this restorative process to allow affected persons to tell their story, so that we can *hear* those stories and then *translate* them into a lesson learned and a change of our culture.

I get phone calls all the time from women who want to speak to me confidentially about their journey. I've also reached out to women whom I know have been harmed, and they've helped me with *my* journey. It's been incredibly rewarding to be entrusted with the stories of people who may not have told them for years and years—who have lost their jobs, their health, and their faith in the system, but are now willing to sit down with us and speak. And we will acknowledge those stories. Then we will work to see what lessons can be applied to the future, so that *everyone*—women and men, people of colour, the LGBTQ+ community, and Indigenous people—can all find a safe, productive place in this organization.

You can't walk away from work like this without being changed, and without being completely respectful of how many people have been so hurt. So as a senior chaplain in the military, I am an advocate for diversity, for equity, and for inclusion. We are stronger when everyone belongs and when there's space at the table for everybody—when all voices matter. Restorative engagement work has really shown me the negative consequences when that *doesn't* happen—when we don't have equal participation at the table, and when some voices are louder than others. When women's voices, especially, are interrupted. I have been the lone woman at many tables. Now that the pathway has been set down, it will be better for people coming up behind me. It's possible now for more people to see themselves doing this.

God doesn't change, but the world does change, and our approach to ministry will necessarily evolve. As the world and our country becomes ever more secular, religious leaders must continue innovating, finding new ways to serve God and meet the needs of God's people. And as chaplains, I think we've done that from the beginning. We've had to learn to quickly adapt, and had to demonstrate to the institution that spiritual life is a vital moral and ethical component of military service that greatly contributes to our resilience and wellbeing. I know I have been stretched in many ways by this ministry, and I really appreciate knowing how far I can go.

Barbara Putnam
Interviewed August 19, 2022 and August 28, 2024

QUESTIONS FOR DISCUSSION AND REFLECTION

1. Barbara encourages every minister to lean on the support of others, "because we really can't do it alone." Who is part of your support network? What is one step you could take to nurture deeper supportive relationships?
2. Chaplaincy work involves listening deeply to the stories of others. What helps or hinders you when trying to be present to someone else's story? What makes you feel like somebody is listening well to *you*?
3. In her various roles, Barbara interacted across different faiths, denominations, cultures, languages, and institutions. What opportunities exist to build bridges across differences in your context? What excites (or worries) you about navigating these kinds of differences?
4. Barbara's ministry story includes many firsts, as she took on leadership roles in a male-dominated environment. Have you ever been in the minority in church, at work, or in your community? What insights and challenges might come along with being "first"?

5

Margo MacDougall

Margo was ordained in 1997 at Morristown Baptist Church in Nova Scotia. In this chapter, she describes her diverse work experiences as a counsellor, a probation officer, college campus staff, and pastor to several Atlantic Baptist churches. Margo reflects on the challenges of serving in ministry as a single woman, describing experiences of sexism and unwelcome attention. Today, her focus is on coaching wounded pastors in order to help restore their sense of calling and confidence in ministry.

My name is Margo MacDougall. I was born in 1962 in Fredericton, New Brunswick.

I was born on a Wednesday, and I believe my mom had me in church the next Sunday. She raised us all to go to church, whether we wanted to or not. And in our family, mostly the girls stuck with it. Knowing my mother's and grandmother's faith really had an influence on me.

My father was a schoolteacher. We moved up to Ontario and stayed there for fourteen years, coming home to New Brunswick every summer. And so when I was eleven, I was in a church service at our home church in Pembroke, Ontario, and a guest speaker was there who gave an invitation to accept Christ. I turned to my mum and said, "Would you go with me?" And she took me by the hand. I accepted the Lord that day, and then there was a baptismal service that evening and I went through the waters of baptism. Communion was also served that night, so I hit all three milestones in one day!

I remember when I was in Ontario, we went without a Sunday school superintendent for several years. There was a woman available, but they told her she wasn't able to do it—she could teach children, but she couldn't lead as the superintendent. That's the first time I realized there was a difference between men and women in ministry, in some people's minds. Some churches didn't want women in leadership, or didn't feel that having women in leadership was biblical. And so, when I felt the Lord calling me into ministry, I knew there would probably be some discussions about that.

I came to a crisis of faith when I was away at Capernwray Bible School. I came to realize that, while I had a full understanding of Jesus as Saviour, I hadn't surrendered. I had accepted salvation, but I hadn't surrendered to the Lordship of Christ. But surrounded by Christians from twenty-three countries, I was overwhelmed by the unity of Christ. We'd sing a song in chapel and it'd be coming out in ten different languages, but it was the same song.

Margo MacDougall

BECOMING A COUNSELLOR

I went to Carleton University in Ottawa for psychology. I wanted to counsel people with what I called "acquired disabilities." At the time, nobody knew what I was talking about, but this is a whole area of research now. It's like if a pianist loses a hand but still has the desire and the need to express herself through piano—I wanted to help people psychologically through that adjustment. So I was in my third year at Carleton and I was saying, "So when do we learn how to counsel people?" And the school said, "Oh, no, Carleton is for research. You should have gone to Ottawa U for counselling!" I was like, "Great, thanks for telling me!"

At the time, I was dating a fellow who was going to Winnipeg to train with the RCMP. I was looking for a master's in counselling, and lo and behold, the only school in Canada at the time that offered a biblical counselling degree at the master's level was Winnipeg Theological Seminary.[1] So I went there from 1985 to 1987. After that, I returned home to New Brunswick and spent a full year looking for work. Not finding any, I went up to Labrador and ran a group home for young offenders, then became a probation officer for adults.

Eventually, a youth counselling job opened up in St. Stephen, New Brunswick, so I moved back home. In St. Stephen, I taught an adult Sunday school class, because they didn't have a teacher. They'd gone without a teacher for two years, and when I offered to teach, they were hesitant because I was a woman. But they agreed, and so I taught that for several years. During that time, I realized that my day job of counselling youth was taking up too much time away from the church ministry that I was really enjoying. And so I interpreted that as the Lord calling me into ministry.

Now, I wasn't sure what type of ministry. Multiple people said, "Oh, you're going to be a youth pastor!" And I said, "No, I don't think so." They said, "Well, you always work with youth!" And I thought, *Oh, I guess I do.*

1. Now Providence Theological Seminary.

In 1993 I went down to Acadia Divinity College (ADC) and spoke with the admissions person. I said I was interested in taking Religious Education to keep my doors open. And he said, "Well, you can study that, but if you got an MDiv, it would keep *all* the doors open: education, pastoral, whatever." And as we talked and prayed, I really felt that was the direction to go, but it wasn't yet with the idea of becoming a pastor.

WE REPRESENT CHRIST'S AUTHORITY

For a long time, I thought about something the apostle Paul had said. This isn't in context, but there's a verse where Paul uses the phrase: "This one thing I do."[2] I was thinking about that and asking God, "OK, Lord, what is the 'one thing I do'? Because I can fill in in a lot of places, but what is the one thing you would have me do?" And I always thought of that in terms of a particular job.

I went to Springforth, which is a youth rally held in the spring in Moncton. The speaker's message was so inspiring that I wrote down: *I want to do this*. Like, I wanted to know how to talk like that, to inspire and strengthen people's faith. But is that teaching? Is that preaching? Is that counselling? What is that? You know, what coat will it wear?

When I interviewed for my license to minister, everything was going along fine. Then, at the end of the interview, one of the deacons I'd known since I was knee-high to a grasshopper said, "Now, what about this 'women in ministry' thing?"

And I said, "Well, I'm glad you asked, because I'm not sure."

He wasn't sure either and said, "I've been in your Sunday school class, so I know the Lord is using you. What do you make of that?"

Again I said, "I don't know what to make of it either. I'm just looking to be a person who is faithful to God's calling. Gender is just what I happen to be—like having brown hair. And so I just want to be faithful." Then I added, "What I would ask if you do

2. Phil 3:13.

grant me this license, and there is ever a time you sense I'm going beyond what the Lord has called me to do, I want any of you to tell me. I also want the church body to feel they are in a position to let me know."

And the deacon said, "Well, that sounds great. That's fine."

That was in the early nineties and I haven't heard from them since, in terms of being on the wrong path or anything.

Later, when I worked at a Bible college, I had one student make an appointment to talk with me. He said he really struggled with me being ordained as a woman. He asked, "What about the authority in the church?" And I said, "Well, the authority isn't a male pastor's authority, or a female's. We represent Christ's authority."

When the student left that conversation with me, he said, "I came in completely against you. I hardly even know you, but I was against you because I knew you were ordained. Now, I'm going out completely supporting you because if it means you're representing Christ's authority, and you're a person trying to be obedient, then there's nothing I can say against that."

I don't feel I'm on a mission to change anybody's mind. I don't think that's part of my calling. I've had the sense from some of my female colleagues that they do feel that's part of their calling: convincing people to allow women to be ordained. But I look at it like, God calls *people* to be ordained. It isn't about letting women be ordained. We let the called of God be ordained.

When I've said that, some people have been quite surprised. Like, "Oh, that's right. It shouldn't be all women; it should be whoever is called by God."

"THEY WERE OPEN TO YOU, OR A CRIMINAL!"

Rev. Judith Tod[3] was at Acadia one time, speaking with the women who were preparing for pastoral ministry. She said, "One thing

3. Judith Tod was interviewed for *Called to Serve*. The episode is available at calledtoserve.ca and on Spotify and Apple Podcasts.

you're going to come across is, if there's a problem, usually people blame the pastor, which is unfortunate. But if it's a *woman* pastor, they will say, 'We're never going to call a female pastor again.' If it's a *male* pastor and there's a problem, they don't say, 'We're never going to call a male pastor again.'"

I don't know why that stuck in my mind, but I remember coming away from that session feeling quite calm in my soul. Although I may encounter difficulties, I won't be the one that has to defend women in ministry.

Then I had an internship with another female pastor about half an hour away, Rev. Sharon Budd[4] in Melvern Square United Baptist Church. Something she really helped me with was the logistics of baptism. I'd never baptized anyone before, and at Acadia, our class had simply gone into the chapel and the professor picked the smallest person to demonstrate and said, "There—that's what you do." When I mentioned this to Sharon, she said, "I'll contact a local church when they're having a baptism and they already have the tank full, and we'll go over and practice."

And that was great, because the last thing you want to do is drown somebody the first time. The first person I baptized was about 6'4" or 6'5" and he was a big man—a huge fella, like a football player type. Two deacons came out with me into the lake as they thought I was going to need help pulling this man up out of the water. But the problem was more getting him *under* the water, because the bigger you are, the more you float! So he popped right back up again. But then the next person I baptized was a lady who was only ninety-eight pounds, and she was one you really had to hold, because if you let go, she'd sink.

When we graduated from Acadia, the regional minister met with each of us to find out what types of churches we felt the Lord would have us minister in. He let us know what churches were currently searching and asked if we wanted our names put forward. So he told me there was one church in particular he thought I would do well at. It was funny—he thought this was so open-minded of

4. Sharon Budd was interviewed for *Called to Serve*. The episode is available at calledtoserve.ca and on Spotify and Apple Podcasts.

him and didn't have any clue how it sounded—but he said, "And I asked this church, 'How would you feel about having an ex-con or a woman as your pastor?' And they were OK with it!"

Now, this could show my prejudice against ex-cons, but I mean, I had been a probation officer, so take that with a grain of salt. But I just thought it was so funny that the regional minister was so excited that "they were open to you, or a criminal!"

THE FIRST THING YOU DO IN A PASTORATE

I graduated with a Master of Divinity in the fall of 1995 and was called to Morristown Baptist, a church in the Annapolis Valley. They'd never had a woman pastor before, and since I was just out of school (even though I was ten years older than most of the graduates), they took me on as an interim pastor. But by May, they were saying they wanted me to stay. I pastored there until 2001.

I was taught that the first thing you do in a pastorate is talk to the local funeral director, because the first death will come when you don't expect it. My first Sunday morning, an hour before I'm supposed to get into the pulpit, I get a phone call. I don't know the person, but it sounds just like a friend of mine, so I figured it was a prank. They said, "So-and-so has just died, and we need you to come in this afternoon and help with the arrangements." I was like, "Uh-huh, uh-huh, and who did you say you were?"

It wasn't a prank. I hadn't really thought through that, as a pastor, I'd be doing funerals, but that's actually the place where I think the Lord used me the most. I'm a procrastinator, and when it comes to funerals, there's no time to procrastinate. You have a short amount of time to get to know the survivors and the life of the person who's gone, and then you sense the Lord giving you a message of comfort as well as an invitation to Christ. When preparing for funerals, I feel reassurance that the Lord has called me to bring the message.

I was ordained in 1997. Examining council was a joy for me. I mean, I wasn't sitting there giddy or anything, but it really confirmed some things. However, in those days, when you finished your education at ADC, you also had an exit interview with the Board of Ministerial Standards. The only question I remember from that was from a lady in Nova Scotia who said, "Now, you're in the pulpit and you're preaching, and you look down and there's a very attractive man in the congregation. What are you going to do?" I wanted so badly to say, "Rip my clothes off and jump the pew!" But I didn't think she knew me well enough to realize how funny that was, so I just said, "Keep preaching!"

I noticed as soon as she asked that question, people looked really uncomfortable. So at the end of my examination, I said, "If it was considered appropriate to ask me that particular question, I'd really encourage you to ask every candidate: whether they're male, female, single, or married. Sometimes we assume that a single person is going to be led into certain temptations more."

The next candidate going in after me was a married fellow I knew, so I told him I wanted to talk to him afterwards because I wanted to know if he was asked the same question. He wasn't, but I think that's because they told the woman who asked that it wasn't appropriate!

I was recommended back to Morristown Baptist for ordination and they were just thrilled. At my ordination service, we sang hymns that had meant a lot to me growing up. I had about ten people come forward for the prayer, each representing different areas in my life—Mum included.

POWER STRUGGLES

Morristown had gone through some difficulties before I got there, and I knew the Lord was using me to help them heal from that. The church developed to the point where they were no longer looking inward but were starting to look outward again for ministry opportunities.

Yet I felt very frustrated, because I wasn't seeing the vision of what the Lord had next. Then the Lord said, "Well, I don't want to hurt your feelings. I don't want you to get all excited about a vision that you're not going to be part of."

I realized, "Oh, OK—he wants me to move on." So I resigned from there in 2001, after six years. I had no idea what I'd be doing next. I was packing my house one day and happened to look outside. I saw the flag on my mailbox went up and had the thought: "Oh, what I'm doing next is in the mailbox." It was an update from Providence that contained an advertisement for a position at Bethany Bible College[5] in Sussex, New Brunswick. So I worked there as a campus counsellor from 2001 until 2011, when five staff were let go due to financial constraints.

At that point, I took on an interim pastoral position at a small Baptist church in New Brunswick. After eight or nine months, they asked me to come on full-time, so I pastored there until I resigned in 2014. That was a strange resignation experience, because I didn't know what the problem was. The animosity from certain individuals was very clear, but the reason for it wasn't. I would rather have resigned after talking things through—even agreeing to disagree—but at least knowing what we were talking about. Even my mum said, "I don't get what's going on. The Lord's called you, and yet people are acting weird and doing strange things and it doesn't make any sense."

I knew there would be conflict in ministry. I don't like it, but I also don't shy away from it because I think we can grow closer together when we commit to resolving conflict. To leave it unresolved is one of the most difficult things for me. I'm an incredibly conscientious person, and part of my personality means it's hard not to carry unresolved things with me. If I can harm someone without realizing it, then how many more times will I harm someone?

I've not returned to full-time pastoring since that experience, but I feel much more healed. It took time, though. I had to go to the doctor and ask for a medical unemployment extension because I was a basket case. I don't know what it is about pastoral ministry that makes people believe it's OK to treat pastors to the point that those kinds of things happen. The power struggles in churches are very damaging and very, very strong.

5. Now Kingswood University.

SINGLENESS AND SEXISM

We had an anniversary service at church once, and I was standing in the kitchen talking to the ladies that were making tea or whatever. And there was a former pastor in the kitchen who came over, put his arm around me, and said, "So what do you think of our girl here?"

I felt like saying, "Get your arm off me. You don't own me. I'm not a girl." But what's difficult is, if you respond in a way that shows you're not appreciative, then it reflects on you. It doesn't reflect on the man being—whatever you want to call that. It felt so condescending to me, and yet those are the kinds of things I always err on the side of letting go. I don't know if women have to let things go like that more than men do, but I can't see someone going up to a male pastor and saying, "What do you think of our boy here?"

I think being a single woman comes into play as well. There are advantages, for sure. For example, when you have free time, that time is more of your own. But there is also the disadvantage that if you are single, people can assume you're available to the church 24/7. I remember asking in a church meeting whether I could post some kind of office hours, or times that are good for people to call. One of the men in that meeting said, "Well, it's a good thing you're not married, because you wouldn't have time to do *anything*!" And I said, "Well, maybe I'm not married because I *don't* have time to do anything."

I was dating a single pastor once, and I noticed that he hardly ever ate at home because he was constantly invited out to people's homes to eat. I think I was invited to someone's home maybe five times over six years. And I mean, a lot of times I was just as happy to be able to go home and cook a quiet meal and spend time on my own to re-energize. But I wondered if, because I'm a single female, people assumed I should be able to cook and clean and all that stuff, and still be at the church 24/7.

Twice that I'm aware of in my ministry, I experienced unwanted attention. Once was from a person in the church who was elderly and married. Whenever we were talking in a group, he would almost always end up beside me and put his arm around me. So that was relatively tame, but it got uncomfortable. I phoned his house one time because I was preaching at an event he was involved with and I needed his feedback. His wife answered the phone and when she handed it to him, I heard her say, "It's your girlfriend." So when the man took the phone, I said, "Oh, sorry, could I just talk to your wife again for a moment?"

She took the phone back and I said, "Just to let you know, it's not his girlfriend; it's the pastor." I wasn't happy to do that, but I really felt she needed to hear that, you know, I don't know what's going on in your home, but I'm the pastor.

Another time, I actually had a fellow stalk me. It was again an older fellow, in his eighties. Like, one morning he called me twenty-six times in two hours. If he saw me in town, he'd follow me by car—or if I was in a grocery store, he'd come and follow me. That was very uncomfortable. He asked me to be involved in his wife's funeral and said to me, "I want you to sit in this chair so that during the funeral, I can sit and look at you." I made sure I sat behind the pulpit so he *couldn't* see me.

I do have one rule that some people think is crazy: I've never travelled with a man alone unless it was my boyfriend and people knew it was. I've had some people tell me that's ridiculous, but any time rumours have gone around that have ruined someone's ministry, they probably didn't plan for that to happen.

One time they held an orientation for new pastors at the CBAC convention office in Saint John. We were supposed to drop off our luggage and then meet at a local church for supper. I had to come over on the boat, so I didn't have a car, and one of the married pastors from Nova Scotia said, "I'll drive you over to supper!"

I said, "Well, I really appreciate that, but I don't think you and I should show up at a motel at four o'clock in the afternoon together in another province." He was like, "Oh my goodness." I still think he thought I was crazy. But then he came to me after supper and said, "You know, I was thinking through what you said. And that's quite smart."

The rumour that would ruin a ministry is usually the one that's not true. I don't know if people even think about it, but I'd rather err on the side of being extra cautious and thought foolish. I think if there's a rumour about a woman, it's considered worse than a rumour about a man, and I just find that no one's going to take a precaution for me so I need to take it for myself. Part of that, too, comes from being sixty and single—you learn to do things for yourself and you don't expect other people to do things for you.

WOMEN IN MINISTRY AREN'T A PLAN B

Over the last ten or twenty years, we've seen more women called into pastoral ministry. And I think that over that same time frame, we've heard more people talk about being wounded or abused by males. People feel more safe to talk about it. And I really think that if the messenger represents someone you can't hear the message from, then you won't hear the message. So I think some of the women God has called into the pulpit are there because there are congregants and people outside the church who couldn't hear the gospel from a man.

Now, I don't think it's a secondary plan to have women. Women in ministry aren't a plan B, as if men were the primary plan but since something happened to their witness, now women are the fallback. I believe that throughout Scripture, God called women into ministry, and they ministered in valid and important and instrumental ways. But I do think that in our current time, there are people who have been deeply wounded, and the Lord would have *everyone* hear the gospel. If you're not able to hear it because of the messenger's exterior, then the messenger needs to change.

In our society, anyway, and in our culture, the female that I am is more able to express my emotions. That's a generalization, because I know many males who can express even better than I, emotionally. But I think we can touch part of the congregation who have been told to be strong their whole life. It's nice to be in the company of a leader who doesn't require you to always have a stiff upper lip.

I also seem to be able to see the ramifications of decisions farther down the line. It may seem like I'm being argumentative at the forefront of an idea, but I can see where it will lead if we choose that route. Sometimes that's a positive and sometimes that's a negative. I've been told I tend to think in a straight line and other people need to move around a bit until they get to that conclusion. So I don't know if that's a female characteristic or a Margo one, with my analytical brain, but many of my male counterparts at seminary took more of the approach of, "Let's just make the decision and let the chips fall where they may."

I AM NOT ASHAMED OF THE GOSPEL

I believe the Lord is calling me now into an online ministry that helps support the healing of wounded pastors. Our convention is desperate to train new pastors, yet we have so many who could be in churches again if they were allowed to heal. When church conflict occurs and everybody appears to be against you, the conscientious pastor is going to ask, "Well, did I misread the call?" Learning how to trust others afterwards is very difficult, because you come to a point where you're not even trusting yourself. There need to be a few key people in a minister's life who recognize God's calling and can help reinforce that.

I'm calling this new initiative Honouring You Ministries (HYM)—I honour God by honouring you. I'm trained as a counsellor, but I'm hoping to offer more of a coaching approach. In the future, I see this ministry branching into other areas like productivity workshops, but right now I want to focus on restoring confidence and a sense of calling in pastors.

One conclusion I internally react against is the assumption that, because I'm ordained, that means I'm a feminist—that I'm anti-male. And that couldn't be further from the truth. That's like saying I'm a frog because I swim in a pond. I recently watched a video online of a woman speaker from Africa. She was talking about the "new feminism" and her definition of feminism was equality. She made some excellent points. But the exposure I've had to feminism is that it's about superiority over men, even to the exclusion of males. When I was in school back in the nineties, I was afraid that people would paint me with that brush.

Over the last while, I've actually been attending an independent Baptist church in Little Lepreau, New Brunswick, which is very fundamental. They know I'm ordained, but they don't ordain women. Yet they are the most supportive and loving church I've been to in a long time. They have a new hymn book, and the hymns are the ones I sang as a child in Ontario. Their singing is very strong. And so it has been a balm to my soul.

I'm very concerned about the lack of men in our churches. As the family and society continue to break down, men's spiritual health really concerns me. The church that I'm currently attending has many godly men who are serving. Now, part of that is because women are not serving in the same way—they teach Sunday school and lead choirs and play the piano—so they are leading, but not in the spiritual sense. But the church seems very pleased I am involved there. The preaching is biblical and includes application as well as scholarship—that idea of, "How do I meet this on the street today?" And every time they pray, there is no hesitancy. In the convention churches I've been at, public prayer by individuals is rare. There was a song I sang in a musical once that comes out of Romans: "I am not ashamed of the gospel, the power of Christ to set us free."[6] And we have a lot of very quiet Christians. We need to become a praying people again.

Margo MacDougall
Interviewed January 26, 2023

6. Rom 1:16.

QUESTIONS FOR DISCUSSION AND REFLECTION

1. Margo held a variety of work positions, both inside and outside the church. What skills and perspectives can those in non-ministry jobs bring to churches and church leadership?
2. Margo served as a single person in ministry and shares some difficult experiences she faced because of that. Have you seen a difference in how ministers are treated because of their relationship status? What assumptions can churches have about people based on whether they are single or married?
3. Margo's current ministry focuses on supporting wounded pastors who have faced things like isolation, power struggles, and unrealistic expectations. What are some ways that congregations might unintentionally hurt their pastors? What things can we do to care for our leaders?
4. Margo describes attending a church she found encouraging, even though it didn't support women's ordination. Did this surprise you? What could other churches learn from this part of Margo's story?

6

Shirley DeMerchant

Shirley was ordained in 1998 at Stevens Road Baptist Church in Dartmouth, Nova Scotia. She was the first person in the CBAC to be specifically ordained to missionary service. In this chapter, Shirley reflects on the inspirational experience she had working as an English-speaking pastor for a South Korean megachurch. She also describes her joyful ministry at Stevens Road, serving as their senior pastor.

MY NAME IS SHIRLEY DEMERCHANT. I was born in 1960, in Perth, New Brunswick.

I grew up in the United Church of Canada, in a church that had female ministers. But it was a very tiny church. There was no Sunday school, so my parents sent me to a Baptist Sunday school down the road. That was where I heard the gospel and responded to it. I was probably eleven or twelve years old at the time.

In high school, I met a lot of other Christians—particularly Baptists. Through them, I found out about the Atlantic Baptist College (ABC)[1] in Moncton. At first I thought, "I don't know if I want to go to a Baptist college." My mother wasn't too keen on it either. She would say, "Those Baptists don't believe in *women*!"

Once I decided that I might be interested in ministry, it was a constant dilemma: should I stay in the United Church that was open to women? But I wasn't moved by the preaching there, and I sometimes felt that—for some ministers—it was more of a job than a calling.

I was more aligned with the theology of the Baptist church, and I really enjoyed the preaching there. But I wondered if I really wanted to go into the Baptist denomination, where it would probably be a struggle for me as a woman.

I wrote to a leader in the United Church with questions about being a minister. I particularly wanted to find out why the United Church said yes to women and the Baptist churches said no. And that leader was very gracious in responding to me: she indicated that pastoral ministry should be an equal opportunity, open to anybody.

But I wasn't satisfied with that. Because for me, the question was: was it biblical? Due to the influence of the Baptist churches, it seemed it wasn't. And yet I struggled with this sense of calling from a very young age. It started with a call to missions: when I was about eight years old, I heard a missionary, and I thought, "Yeah, I could go—I could be a missionary!"

So I felt this call, but I wasn't sure what it would be *to*. After talking to my Baptist friends about ABC, I thought it would be

1. Now Crandall University.

good to have a Baptist foundation. And I wanted to go to a small school. So I studied at ABC from 1978 to 1980.

Those two years were tremendous for me. The fellowship and teaching were quite significant in forming my understanding of what it meant to be a Christian. I really wasn't sure where I was heading as far as a career, though. I wrote in my journal then: *Lord, are you calling me into full-time Christian ministry?*

It took a long time to get an answer to that question.

I was interested in missions and knew I needed to get a good education before I could apply to any mission organization, so I went to Acadia University to finish my Bachelor of Arts. It wasn't until just a couple months before I graduated that I felt drawn to Acadia Divinity College (ADC).

I remember appearing before the Board of Ministerial Standards—back then, first-year students would meet with them, and then before you graduated, you met with them again. One of the questions they always asked is, "Tell us what you're called to do. Where are you heading?"

And all I could say was, "I'm called to be here."

GENDER SHOULDN'T BE AN ISSUE

I went to Acadia University from 1980 to 1982, and then took my Master of Divinity at ADC from 1983 to 1985. At ADC, I think all of my professors were male, and they were such godly, humble men. The strength of the college at that time was in training preachers—and I am so grateful for that, because that's one of my strengths. I really enjoy preaching.

Some female students seemed to be at the college trying to prove that women were as good as men—no, that women were better than men. And the pulpit was one place for them to prove it. I found that really offensive, and when I saw that, I determined that I was not going to make my gender an issue. I'm not a competitive person. If God wants me in ministry, he's going to have to open up the opportunities, because I'm *not* going to go pounding on doors saying, "Because I'm a woman and the Bible says women can do this, I should be in the pulpit!"

If there were going to be any conflicts in my ministry, I didn't want it to be because of gender. I can't do a thing about my gender. If a church doesn't want me, I don't want to be there. Ministry is hard enough when you *have* the support of the people. If you don't have their support, that's a really hard way to start.

Being a female student wasn't a big issue for me. Except once in a while you'd have conversations with people who said that women shouldn't be in the pulpit. And sometimes I felt like when a male student would walk through the doors of a church, our congregations were silently clapping—like, "Here's a man for ministry, ready to serve our churches!" When a woman walked through, it felt more like, "I wonder if she reads her Bible?" Overall, though, I don't remember having any really difficult conversations with my classmates, and the professors at ADC were very supportive.

The people who nurtured me most, actually, were men. Even with InterVarsity Christian Fellowship (IVCF), we had a tremendous male staffer. I was involved with IVCF as a student, and they tried very hard to have both men and women working together. That's the best scenario: working together. Gender shouldn't be an issue.

SOMETHING I'D BEEN WANTING TO HAPPEN

Just before I graduated, I got a phone call from IVCF, asking if I'd consider being a staff worker in St. John's, Newfoundland. I thought, "Great! I can work with students!" InterVarsity had been such an influence in my life, giving me grounding in how to lead small groups, and in evangelism. I was really happy to offer students what had been so beneficial to me.

And going overseas didn't look like it would happen anytime soon. I had gone to Urbana, a major missions conference, and there was a mission organization I wanted to check out. I was so disappointed when they said, "We can't take you until you pay off your student loan."

So I went to St. John's for three years with InterVarsity, raising my own support. I really loved working with students and teaching the Bible, but I realized it wasn't financially sustainable and ended up coming back to Nova Scotia.

A job opportunity came up to be Director of Christian Education at Stevens Road United Baptist Church in Dartmouth. I was hired on and worked in that role from 1989 to 1992. Don Krause was the senior pastor there, and he wanted to serve in the military as a chaplain in Bosnia for six months. So he called me into his office and asked if I would fill in as interim senior pastor. I agreed, because it was only going to be for six months while he was gone. But I said, "It has to be unanimous. I'm not going to let gender be an issue. Everyone at Stevens Road must be in agreement that this is a good idea."

So it went before the church. It probably helped that there weren't many other options because it was only for six months—and the church already knew me as their Christian education director. And so we agreed, and it was a tremendous experience! I really felt that if I had tried to fail, the church would not let me fail. It was like, "We're all in this together," and our goal was just, "Let's keep the church doors open until this man comes back!"

But what happened in that time was something I'd been wanting to happen. I had both men and women take me aside during those six months and say, "You really should find a church to pastor because you have gifts for pastoral ministry." That meant so much to me, because I had developed a sense of the importance of affirmation by the body of Christ—the local congregation. In fact, when I graduated from ADC, I'd decided I wasn't going to seek ordination immediately, because I wanted that affirmation from other people first. We don't see ourselves the way others see us.

And so when Don came back to Stevens Road, I decided I would put my name out there to pastor a church. I contacted the CBAC area minister and I didn't get one interview. Talk about confusing!

I didn't know what to do. I had to pay bills. My student loan was still a concern. But *nothing*—absolutely nothing—came up.

Then I found out about teaching English overseas and I thought, "You know what, if I did that, I could probably make enough money in one year to pay off my student loan. And then I can go back to that mission organization." I had no overseas experience yet, so it was also a kind of a test to see if I could survive in a foreign country with different foods and culture.

So I signed a contract to teach English abroad in South Korea. I thought, "I'll go overseas for a year." And then I stayed for ten!

HOSANNA PRESBYTERIAN CHURCH

I was in South Korea from 1996 to 2007. I found many opportunities to do ministry there. I had decided that I didn't need to be ordained to do ministry; I didn't need anyone's permission. I could do ministry wherever.

So I was in South Korea for about six weeks, attending a Korean church in Busan that had an English worship service. It's called Hosanna Presbyterian Church. After six weeks, the missionary in charge of that service was in another country and had a heart attack. Someone needed to take his place providing the English service, and because I had theological training, the church asked, "Would you do it?"

I preached in Korea for almost all of the ten years I was there. By the time I left, Hosanna Church had grown to thirteen thousand people! They built a parking lot with three levels of underground parking. They had services in five different languages besides Korean. They had dawn prayer meetings, starting at 5 a.m. People would come at *5 a.m.* to church—showered, shampooed, and suited up for a ten-hour workday. They would run past you on the sidewalk to get a good seat in the church at 5 a.m.!

At these prayer meetings, people were invited to come kneel up on the platform if they wanted a pastor to pray for them. There were about twenty-five assistant pastors and I was the only female, but the senior pastor insisted I participate in the prayers.

So I went up and prayed, in English, because my Korean was very poor. And after doing that once or twice, I stopped. When someone asked me why I stopped praying for the Koreans, I said, "I can only pray in English! They should have someone who can pray for them in Korean." And this person said to me, "Shirley, most of our pastors pray in tongues anyway!"

It was the most dynamic church I've ever been part of. It was my first experience with the Presbyterian Church, and it profoundly impacted me. I used to cry all the way through the Wednesday night service. I couldn't speak Korean very well, but I could read it, and some of the worship songs I know today are ones I first knew in Korean.

The senior pastor at Hosanna was amazing. His name was Pastor Cho. He had such a vision. Like he wanted to develop the church's ministry to handicapped people, so he hired a pastor who was physically handicapped. He wanted to develop a ministry to seniors, so he hired a pastor who was a senior citizen. And he wanted *me* on staff because I was a native English speaker in charge of the English-speaking worship service.

Some of the Koreans told me later that one of the reasons he also wanted me on staff was to help open the eyes of the congregation to women in pastoral ministry. They found it really fascinating to see a woman doing things they only saw a male pastor do.

For example, a couple of men at the English service wanted to be baptized, but only the senior pastor in the Korean church did baptisms. So I went to the senior pastor and I asked, "Can I baptize these two men?" And his question was, "In Canada, would you be able to baptize?"

I said yes, so he said OK. It was the same for doing communion, and even weddings. Because the church in Canada would allow me, his attitude was, "OK, I guess you can do it here."

ORDAINED TO MISSIONARY SERVICE

After being in Korea for a year, I thought, "You know, I won't be here forever. When I go back home, it'd be really helpful if I was ordained. That would open up doors." So while I was overseas, I decided to seek ordination for my future, for when I would return to Canada.

I contacted Harry Gardner[2] and told him I'd like to be examined by the ordination council. And he said, "Great! We'll see what we can do to make it happen." But then I said, "I've got a teaching contract, so I'll need to come back to Korea afterwards."

Harry said, "Oh, that could be a problem if you're not staying in Canada, because the CBAC ordains people to ministry in Canada." He told me he'd look into it and see what we could do.

According to the rules, you can be ordained to different areas of ministry—like pastoral ministry or chaplaincy, sort of like choosing a specialty—but then you aren't restricted to that ministry. Once you're ordained, you're ordained. So Harry got back to me and said, "I think we can ordain you to missionary service, because that's what you're doing in the Korean church."

When I went before the examining council, Dr. MacRae introduced me.[3] He said, "Shirley, you're unique in a couple of ways. One is, you will be the first person in our convention ordained to missionary service." The CBAC had sent lots of missionaries, but I guess no one had gone that route of being *ordained* to missionary service. And secondly, Dr. MacRae said, "You're the only candidate we have of no fixed address."

I was coming from Korea, then was going to be in Halifax for a while before the interview—but my home was in New Brunswick. So that made it a little bit complicated.

I think my situation made it easier for me to pass. At the time I went for ordination, it was really hard for women. Even if you were the perfect female candidate, you *could not* get 100 percent in the voting, because any associations who weren't in favour of female pastors told their delegates, "You have to vote no if there's a female candidate."

I remember one person in particular asked me several questions, and because I could say, "Well, I'm going back to Korea," that

2. Harry Gardner was the executive minister for Atlantic Baptists.

3. As principal of Acadia Divinity College, Andrew MacRae was the chief examiner on the examining council.

seemed to make his questions irrelevant. I don't know if people felt threatened when a female candidate came forward or what. But this guy didn't seem to feel so threatened because I wasn't going to be pastoring a church in Atlantic Canada.

I appeared before the examining council in 1997, but due to my teaching contract, I couldn't be ordained until 1998. My family came to my ordination service at Stevens Road, and it was wonderful. There's something really profound about the laying on of hands, and people coming together just to affirm your gifts. I remember afterwards, standing in the gym where the reception was, and I turned to my sister and said, "This is just like a wedding!" She looked at me and said, "Well, there's something missing here." So she didn't quite agree, but it's the closest thing I ever had!

Two women in the congregation went together on a gift for me, and it was a portable communion set. I have used that communion set so many times in hospitals, giving communion to dying people.

WHAT'S GOOD FOR THE CHURCH

Pastor Cho really opened up a lot of doors in ministry for me. I could have stayed in Korea a long time. But in 2007 I came back to Canada permanently, because I felt it was time to be closer to my parents as they were getting older.

I returned to the Halifax area and once again attended Stevens Road. Whenever I had visited from Korea, they would ask me to speak, so we always kept in touch. I returned there and waited for God to open some doors. I was looking for a position where I could focus on missions, ministry to singles, and small groups.

While I was looking for opportunities, the senior pastor at Stevens Road resigned. Months went by before the church asked me to consider being a candidate. So I said, "Look, I will be interim pastor while you look for somebody, but I'm not interested in being a senior pastor." So I became interim pastor there again. And because I knew it was a temporary position, I found I could preach some really hard sermons about the need to change—because this church was so traditional, in so many ways. I thought, "I've got nothing to lose—if they fire me, I'm just here temporarily!"

Well, as I ministered to the congregation, people responded. One charter member especially would say, "Shirley, we *really* needed that sermon." And my heart began to change. Finally, I went to the head of the search committee and said I'd like to put my name forward to be considered in their interviews.

Well, then we had to tell the church: "We're going to have a church meeting to vote on a candidate." And the church was in an uproar! They said, "We haven't even heard that person preach! We don't know who we're going to be voting on! What are the deacons doing?" And because I couldn't tell them I was the candidate, all I could say was, "You need to trust the deacons. Just go to the meeting."

People laughed when they got to the meeting and found out it was me they were voting on. I did tell the search committee there had to be 100 percent support for me to accept the job. And everyone agreed. So, I became the senior pastor.

But I knew not *everybody* at the church agreed with women pastors. There was one dear lady in that congregation—I was often in her home, and she would feed me—a godly woman. I heard she was at the meeting, and yet there was a 100 percent vote in favour.

So a couple of days later, I went to her house and said, "I know that you don't agree with women pastors, yet the church voted me in?" And she said, "Shirley, I'm a member of this church. What's good for the church, I vote for."

How un-Baptist! I have not met many Baptists who vote according to what's good for the *body* and to maintain the unity of the body. So many Baptists, in my experience, want to express their own opinion. And they cause a lot of division. So I had so much respect for this woman, and she continued to be very supportive.

I remember talking to the chairman of the Deacons' Board one day while we were working on the agenda for a deacons' meeting. I was complaining that the church was so resistant to change. And he blinked two or three times, and one eyebrow went up—and I said, "Why are you reacting that way?" He said, "We have a female senior pastor!"

I'd gotten so comfortable in that church that I kind of forgot how unique that was! It was quite an exceptional church.

One of my highlights there as senior pastor was "supervising" (if I can use that word) field education for Dr. Joyce Ross. Joyce was ordained when she was seventy-five.[4] So when I say "supervise," I was supervising a woman much older than me, with much more life experience. But she was in a situation where she wanted to go for ordination, and there wasn't any Black church where the pastor was able to supervise her. I just happened to meet her at the Atlantic Baptist Women convention when she was looking for a place.

So this is an older Black woman—and with our Black communities, we got together for things like the World Day of Prayer, but we didn't do a lot of things together. Their church expression is quite different than ours—much more lively, for one thing.

And Joyce said, "I can't be ordained until I find a church where I can do my supervised field education." And so I said, "I'll ask—you could probably do it at our church!" I expected our deacons would be in favour, but I didn't realize the impact she would have.

Joyce is a dignified lady—she always wore a matching hat with her outfit. She had so much joy and so much wisdom, and people loved to hear her pray. For a whole year, we had her at our church. We would go on visits together, and she'd preach and participate in everything. I would not have been able to go into a Black church and do as well as she did in our church, and the people loved her.

Actually, when she was interviewed at the examining council, one man was so impressed by her that he put his hand up and asked, "Dr. Ross, may I ask you a question? Would you be our pastor?" She is a delightful woman, and a godly prayer warrior. Watching my church go through the experience of supervising a woman who is older, from a different culture and different life experience—that was a highlight for all of us. We were just so proud

4. See chapter 12.

of her, and she connected so well with our congregation, which at that time was probably 100 percent White. That was pretty special.

THE WISDOM OF THE BODY

It was really hard to leave Stevens Road. I was there from 2007 to 2015. But I decided to go when I saw that my parents needed greater support from me, so I moved in with them in Woodstock, New Brunswick. I'm not working full time now, but I am doing pulpit supply every Sunday.

There were times in my ministry when I felt really lonely. Like when I would go to a ministerial meeting and I was the only female around the table. But what I found even more difficult was being single in ministry. Ministry is really tough and it's hard to be balanced. It's hard to sift through criticism and vision and perspective when you're by yourself. Couples who work effectively in ministry together have help—like, even someone to help carry stuff from the trunk into the church, as well as someone to say, "You know, you're overreacting!"

I had a few married friends who were really good. Like this one couple: they would invite me out to their house for supper on Friday night. I had to do youth group for a while on Friday nights, so I would complain about the youth group and how I didn't want to go. Then they'd check their watch: "OK, Shirley, time for youth group!" They knew enough to let me spout off my frustration and not be afraid that I was going to quit.

I have a really good single friend as well. We started coffee time after church so that people always had some place to go right afterwards if they wanted to connect. Then we started what we called "Lunch Bunch" for anyone who wanted to go eat together after coffee time. I made that a priority because that way I connected with people over food after the service, and it was great for visitors. Widows would come, or couples would say, "Look, we didn't take anything out of the freezer, so we're going to Lunch Bunch." That was really helpful.

So I had some good friends. But I think it's really hard to do ministry alone. I learned the importance of team ministry: not trying to do it all yourself, and finding people who can do the things you can't. Especially where I could not consider myself a "team," being single, I really learned to depend on other people.

I believe we need to strengthen our relationships and listen to one another, seeking the wisdom of people outside of ourselves—the wisdom of the body. Like with my deacons, I would tell them, "There are more of you than there are of me, so you are my ears. Listen to the congregation and let me know the things I need to hear." And I really valued their feedback. If I came up with a great idea and the deacons said, "Hm, that's not such a great idea," then I trusted them! I thought it was really foolish to go against your deacons. I think that protected me from making a lot of mistakes.

I wish every church could have a male and female in pastoral leadership, whether they were a married couple or not. There's not just strength in numbers; God created us male and female. And to me, the best combination is to do ministry together, male and female. I've seen that work really well.

PEOPLE DO CHANGE

The Baptist church where I was influenced so much as a young person was not in favour of women ministers. But two or three years ago, they called and asked me if I would fill in, because they needed pulpit supply for one Sunday. I couldn't believe it. Before we hung up, I said, "You do know I'm a woman?" And the guy calling said, "Yup, yeah, I do know!"

And it was a great experience. People *do* change, and we need to give them credit for that. When I was there, I said, "This is a good chance for me just to say thank you, church. Because when I was a teenager, you were there. And you gave me a really good grounding in the Scriptures." I took the opportunity to say, "You know, when you open your doors to young people, you never know the impact you're going to have on them."

So I was very well received. Some people do change.

And I often look back and think, "Wow, God, you've really taken me on this incredible journey: from this community of 350 people to being in this big Korean church, and then a senior pastor. I would never have dreamt that even possible."

I did inspire one person. I remember after a baptism service at our church, there was this little girl—elementary age. After the baptism service, she said, "Wow, when I grow up, I want to be a baptizer!" So you just never know.

Shirley DeMerchant
Interviewed July 8, 2022

QUESTIONS FOR DISCUSSION AND REFLECTION

1. Shirley grew up in a denomination where she saw women ministers. How did the roles *you* saw for men and women growing up shape your ideas about what you could do? How might you be influencing others' perceptions of gender roles today, intentionally or not?
2. Shirley describes intentionally waiting for affirmation from her community before she pursued ordination. How important do you think it is for churches to identify people with pastoral gifts? Who are potential future leaders you see in your church?
3. According to Shirley, the senior pastor at Hosanna Presbyterian Church "wanted to develop the church's ministry to handicapped people, so he hired a pastor who was physically handicapped. He wanted to develop a ministry to seniors, so he hired a pastor who was a senior citizen." Is the diversity of your community reflected in its leadership? How could your church become a better community for people of multiple ethnicities, ages, and ability levels?

4. Shirley believes that "gender shouldn't be an issue" and prefers when both men and women work together. Have you seen this kind of collaborative environment before? How might leaders intentionally nurture more collaborative environments?

7

Diane Juckes

Diane was ordained in 2003 at Newcastle United Baptist Church in New Brunswick. Much of her ministry has focused on hospital and prison chaplaincy. In this chapter, Diane describes returning to faith through her journey of addiction recovery. She shares stories of motorcycle ministry with her husband, prison ministry in a maximum-security setting, and the challenges and opportunities presented to her as a chaplain in a multi-faith context.

My name is Diane Juckes. I was born in 1955 in Campbellton, New Brunswick.

I grew up in a home where there was a discussion around believing in God, and in love, but that wasn't displayed. It wasn't felt. One of my parents would participate in activities throughout the weekend (as I eventually began to do) and then sit in church on Sunday, hungover, yet trying to fit in. I totally abandoned going to church from the time I graduated until I got clean and sober at thirty years of age. I left simply because I felt that a lot of people—including me—were sitting in the church pews trying to look holy while leading very unholy lives. That really put a bad taste in my mouth.

I wandered away from the faith for a number of years and felt so distant from God. I know it was my shame and embarrassment that caused that. I fully own that God didn't ever go away—I was the one who moved away from him.

My return to faith happened in California. My future husband and I went to a tiny congregational church there in Torrance. Our relationship was founded in a recovery program and in a new walk with the Lord together. That church felt like home and had very caring, loving people. They met not only on Sundays but throughout the week for Bible study and events at lunchtime and in the evening. Their home life, church life, and work life all matched who they were representing, and I thought, "Wow, that is so impressive." That church gave us an amazing opportunity to put ourselves out there and be embraced.

At thirty-two, I was diagnosed with bowel cancer. I had a resection of my bowel, eight months of chemotherapy, and twenty-five radiation treatments. And during all that, I desperately missed my family, especially my mom. When my husband, Michael, heard how homesick I was, he said, "I'm going to pack you up and move you to Canada so we can be with your family." So that's what we did. When my recovery process was done, we returned to the Campbellton area in New Brunswick and Michael became a Canadian citizen.

WE JUST WEREN'T CAUGHT AND CHARGED

When we were in California, we'd begun a little motorcycle ministry, riding for Christ while clean and sober, with patches on our backs. Michael was mostly the initiator of that—in all honesty, he's much smarter than I am, and he's got more doctorate degrees to prove it! He's just very wise. I felt the bike club was more of his calling, but I got a Harley-Davidson—not to be outdone of course!

In New Brunswick, Michael wanted to continue riding his Harley as a representative for the Lord, so we started doing prison ministry. By that point, we'd had a few years of solid teaching under our belts, but more importantly we wanted to exhibit the life and love of Christ to those who were struggling in prison. That's what God laid on both of our hearts.

We started riding to the jails in Edmunston and Bathurst, and to the Dalhousie Regional Correctional Centre. We'd bring the inmates a short message from the Word, as well as lots of love and words of encouragement. We shared our story of recovery: how we became clean and sober and established a life in the Lord, and how that made such a resounding difference in our lives. One thing we've always said is that Michael and I have done things in our lives that we just weren't caught and charged with. Some of those guys have been discovered for whatever their crimes were and have been locked up, but there's lots of folks who have committed crimes and just haven't been caught. So we let the inmates know there was no judgement from us. In God's eyes, sin is sin, and we're all on the same playing field. God considers us all equal, and he loves us.

One day when we were travelling down to the Atlantic Institution in Renous, God laid it on our hearts simultaneously that we were to sell our home and move to Miramichi to do visits at the youth prison and the men's maximum-security facility. We had confirmation of God's voice because when Michael and I stopped to have lunch, I said, "God spoke to me while we were riding." And Michael said, "He spoke to me, too." We were amazed at how awesomely God moves, and there wasn't any question whether or not we would do it.

THE GREAT INQUISITION

When we got home, we put our house on the market and moved down to Miramichi in 2000. Michael and I became members of the Newcastle United Baptist Church there, now known as The Point. They gave me my license for ministry. That year, I also began formal education. I took classes for the Canadian Association for Pastoral Practice and Education (CAPPE),[1] which were required by a lot of the chaplaincy organizations. Dr. Charlie Taylor was teaching CAPPE then at Acadia, and he was like the Baptist guru (pardon the term) of pastoral education. If anyone says they were taught by Charlie Taylor, all the other old folks in the room will go, "Wow!"

To pursue ordination, I also needed to take a class on Baptist polity. I entered that class about two weeks late and was trying to play catch-up, not coming from a Baptist background. I'd go week to week thinking, "These people are going to think I'm the village idiot, because I know nothing." When they'd ask for classroom participation, I felt really uncomfortable. However, with lots of studying I earned my bachelor's and master's, and eventually a doctorate in ministry through a school in Alabama.

I was ordained in 2003. I've referred to my being ordained and standing before the examining council as my being at the Great Inquisition. I found it overwhelming standing in the presence of all those scholarly folks. It was intimidating, though not because they wanted it to be. As a matter of fact, the minister who prayed over me for peace and comfort before I went in was such a doll. She reminded me: "You know, Diane, everybody's here today to support you. You wouldn't have made it this far if we didn't have faith in you. We are your friends: we are for you, not against you."

1. Now the Canadian Association for Spiritual Care.

I thought God gave her the exact words I needed to hear to somewhat squelch those terrible feelings of inadequacy I had.

My ordination service was one of the holiest moments in my life. It was such validation—that God would consider me called apart to serve. It was like he said, "See, Di? You didn't make all this up in your head." All my siblings came and supported me. And my mom, who couldn't have been a stauncher Catholic, was so proud of me and my stick-to-itiveness. She recognized the challenges I'd had in life and knew it was by God's grace and help that I managed to overcome. When she later passed away, I did her funeral.

Some of the folks in my congregation wanted to make sure I understood they were ordaining me to *prison* ministry, as opposed to pastoral ministry. That actually wasn't the case—my ordination papers clearly say I've been ordained to pastoral ministry. But I think some of the men might have been afraid I'd go and apply at their church!

PRISON MINISTRY AT THE ATLANTIC INSTITUTION

I pastored at the Lower Derby Baptist Church for ten years, and was simultaneously the Protestant chaplain at the Miramichi Regional Hospital during that time. I've now been at the Atlantic Institution in Renous for ten years, seven of which have been full-time.

Chaplaincy at the hospital is a totally different animal than chaplaincy in a maximum men's institution. At the men's institution, I am the site chaplain overseeing two hundred men, and that group includes around five Jewish men, forty Muslims, twelve Wiccans, some Buddhists, a Hindu, one Satanist—and there's a Rastafarian in there too. There's a myriad of different faith groups I oversee. And so I certainly can't provide something like a Buddhist service, but there's a Buddhist I connect with monthly who provides calls and comes into the prison. The same goes for the imam, and the Roman Catholic deacon who comes in. So I'm overseeing all those ministries and making sure those guys are in every month, doing their thing and connecting with people. I also help meet everybody's needs for prayer and counselling, and I provide services and do hospital visits when men are in the hospital after an altercation.

I've been taken hostage once. That was an amazing experience. Praise the Lord—myself and another chaplain who was in there with the inmate were able to talk him down after an hour and a half. But we had guns at the ready outside the door. His whole thing was that he was going to kill the other woman who was in the room with us and was going to keep me hostage. I thought, "Well, that's a bonus—at least he's not going to kill me!" But anyway, I made a phone call and told the guys outside the door to stand down, because the inmate was willing to go. He was a schizophrenic and not medicated and he'd had a psychotic break. He's now on medication and I've had him come to the chapel and had some really good visits with him. He's left the Muslim faith and become a Christian, so the whole thing has just flipped itself on its head. God is a restorer.

Some of the inmates are big, and tall, and I'm not tall. I'm probably 5'4" now. And I'm so fragile because I've got a pacemaker and I'm almost seventy, so I've got all kinds of bone ailments and I'm not in the best of health. The inmates know they could do some serious damage very quickly with me. Yet any time they try and intimidate me, I just nicely give it right back. I say, "Listen, buddy, the worst thing you think you can do to me is kill me, and I will just go to be with Jesus. So even if you kill me, I'm not losing out." My faith is so great that they can't really lord anything physically over me, and that makes them reconsider. Not so much that they're thinking, "Oh, this chick is tough," but more like, "Her faith is so great."

Prison can be a frightening place. And yet, we don't have cameras or recording machines in the chapel, because we chaplains thought the inmates should have a safe space. Even if that means being taken hostage—at least the inmates know they have a place where their conversations aren't being monitored. And so the windows to the chapel can all open and there are gun ports.

Last night, I stayed at work late because one of our inmates got news that his teenage sister died of an overdose and he was devastated. He came to the chapel and had a difficult time looking at me face-to-face. I'm old enough to be his grandma, and so when he was weeping, I got up from my chair at the table and walked around to give him a big bear hug. I said, "I want you to know you're not alone. It's OK to cry. This is a safe place."

That was so meaningful to him. This inmate's parents were both drug addicts and he grew up not feeling loved. From time to time, his siblings were split up, and it was so difficult. I really felt it made sense that he was starved for love, so I let him know that God loved him and that I loved him in Christ's love. I told him I will check back on him to see if he's been able to connect with family and how he is processing. He used that word—he said, "My mom is having a hard time processing." And I thought, "No kidding. Your child is not supposed to die of an overdose in their youth." So in the midst of all this sadness, what can I bring to the table as a chaplain? And that's to listen, and to love him.

THE FEMINIST CARD

I didn't know there had been any female Baptist clergy in New Brunswick up in this neck of the woods. At one point I read of a female Baptist minister in the Derby area and I was so encouraged by that. I hope when I get to heaven I get to meet this woman, because, you know that story about the Little Engine That Could? The train who says, "I think I can, I think I can!" Hearing about that woman resonated so deeply within me that I thought, "I can do that. I can do that."

Even when there are a few disdaining voices, that encouragement helps push me along. Some folks are still really entrenched in the idea that women should have no place or say, not taking into account that when the Scriptures were written, women weren't educated and the social context was different. I mentioned there were some men who weren't really supportive of my being ordained. Sadly, I think that attitude causes a lot of pain. I feel a sense of sadness for the men who are like that, because I think it's probably difficult at home for their wives. If you're making it known how you feel about women, there are probably some underlying difficulties.

I don't hear that negativity from God. He clearly called me into ministry, so I just ask those men, "Did God make a mistake?" But that's been a challenge. And it's funny, because I talked about these issues yesterday at prison—about feminism, because there's a lot of women guards. Are they perceived as being forceful and in competition with men? And for me, in my area of work—is there a sense that I have to be a feminist? That I am in competition with men, or have an "overlording" sense of power?[2]

That's what I see in the feminist movement. And I may be all wrong—I may be putting too much weight on how they present themselves. But I believe women are to be treated equally and we're not to be subservient. That's what's worked so well for my husband and me over the lifetime we've been together.

Michael knows I'm his helpmate. That's what Scripture says. However, he is also *my* helpmate. He also helps me. It's a win-win situation. Some days I may be giving 80 percent and him 20 percent, some days we may both be giving 50 percent, and sometimes we're both giving 100 percent. But whatever the case, we consider one another as equals. We're not holding back what could be our best—I guess that's really the heart of the matter.

My husband's servant heart is as deep as mine, and God could not have given me a better man to be in ministry with. He's a wonderful, loving husband and father. So for me, I haven't had to apply or draw on the feminist card, just because I am so well loved and embraced.

HOW DOES INCLUSIVITY PLAY OUT?

In the prison system, there's been one lad who probably stands around 6'4", and he looks just like Moses to me. He's not at Atlantic

2. See 1 Pet 5:3 and Matt 20:25.

Institution anymore, and I've got to tell you, I really miss him. He probably gets around three hours of sleep a night and is able to function on it. He'd do some cleaning work for a nominal pay—like maybe five dollars every two weeks—and then the rest of the time, he was in the Word. He reads and studies literally night and day.

I remember when I began at the prison, he was really crotchety with me. He'd be so short and nasty and hover over me, as if to bring home the point. But you know, we came to love and respect one another. He stopped coming to chapel partway through my tenure—not because of me, but because the sacred space has had everything taken down. Like, the cross has had to come down. I've got a thing hidden of the Last Supper, tucked away in a place that I hope will be less noticeable. When some of these "icons" or paintings or whatever all started coming down, he said to me, "You're sterilizing the sacred space!" And I said, "It's got to be inclusive. It has to be a friendly space for all."

If you want to work at the hospital or the prison or anything government-based as a chaplain, things have changed. They really have sterilized the chapel. Someone had suggested we bring in things for pagan ceremonies, and so not going *that* route meant taking everything else down so it's all on an equal playing field, so to speak. The government says if you want to have space, it's got to be all-inclusive. So at the chapel on some Fridays, I call down the Muslim men to be in the sacred space for Jummah prayer. I'm not in there *with* them, but they have access to that space.

For me, that's been a huge challenge. The cross was taken down when I was the chaplain at the hospital, and there was a big uprising in the community about it. I know that Canada is inclusive and we are focused on the inclusion of all people, but for Christians it feels more *exclusive*, so it's really bittersweet. It's a conflict that needs to be resolved—how does inclusivity play out?

I remember at the beginning when all this transpired, I thought, "I am going to lose my mind. This is such a hard one to try and walk through and navigate!" It was really tough for me because of the feedback in the community—and truly, how I felt, too. However, I've come to recognize the value of being all-inclusive, and I've found a softening in my own spirit that allows me not to have that tension today which I initially had.

CHRISTMAS PARTIES WITH THE INMATES

One of the biggest blessings in prison is that it doesn't matter if you're a Jew, a Muslim, a pagan, a whatever—in December, we have Christmas parties with the inmates. I have volunteer groups who come up from Nova Scotia and we sing and play games and do puzzles and fellowship things. There's a devotional message that's brought, which speaks clearly about Christ. And all those other faiths are there. Yet, it's about fellowship and love, you know? The fellowship that comes from loving them.

I gather up forty dozen sweets from churches in the community that believe in our ministry, and I cart those in at the beginning of Advent. We embrace all the faith groups who choose to come out, and let them hear the Word. Then we let the Spirit of God move in them. We always pray before the service, "Lord, open their ears and open their eyes, that they would see Jesus." And then after they've gone, we pray, "Lord, now that they've gone back to their homes, please move. We just count on you moving." And we leave it with God.

Nobody's there saying, "Oh, this Jesus guy—what a joke!" Nobody is disrespectful. It's the most wonderful thing: guys who can be such turnips to the guards and can be so disrespectful come down to the chapel and are as meek as lambs. These men—grown, burly, old and young, faith aside—laugh until they're crying and grabbing their stomachs because they're having so much fun.

When you speak at Christmastime of joy, and hope, and love, and peace—I only wish we could film the prison chaplaincy program, because it's life-changing. For anybody who wants to consider prison ministry and see a side of it that nobody ever hears about: that is it. It's a call to serve and not a job.

Diane Juckes
Interviewed December 13, 2023

QUESTIONS FOR DISCUSSION AND REFLECTION

1. How does Diane's ministry journey challenge your stereotypes about who can be a pastor or what ministry looks like?
2. Have you ever considered being involved with prison ministry? How could your church better support ministry to inmates and connect with local prison chaplains?
3. Diane describes being enormously challenged at first by the requirements of ministry in a multi-faith context. What opportunities does a multi-faith environment provide for ministry? What parts do you find challenging?
4. Some inmates perceived Diane as a trustworthy, grandmother-like figure. Others saw her as potentially weak because of her height, gender, and age. How do you think others perceive you? Are there ways you want to serve your community that others might not expect?

8

Sherrolyn Riley

Sherrolyn was ordained in 2003 at Victoria Road Baptist Church in Dartmouth, Nova Scotia. She has also pastored at a small rural church in Mahone Bay. In this chapter, Sherrolyn describes entering seminary after her retirement and persevering in ministry in spite of discouragement and depression. She also describes the differences she found between pastoring in predominantly White and Black congregations.

Sherrolyn Riley

My name is Sherrolyn Riley. I was born in Halifax, Nova Scotia.

My family was very church-oriented. In fact, my grandfather was once pastor of the church we went to, Victoria Road United Baptist in Dartmouth. And my grandmother, Muriel States, was very involved in all the women's work. She was actually the official organizer for our African United Baptist Association, and she organized sixteen different women's auxiliaries as well as two men's brotherhoods across twenty-three churches.

My mother was also very active in the church. She played the organ, led in the Baptist Young People's Union, and was a leader for Canadian Girls in Training (CGIT), an ecumenical girls' group founded in 1915. CGIT was very much like Girl Guides, but faith-based. We had a fourfold purpose: to cherish health, seek truth, know God, and serve others. At one point there were around twenty-five CGIT groups in Baptist churches across the Maritimes, but the program started to fizzle out in the 1980s.

As a young person, I was very shy and withdrawn, but being a CGIT leader helped give me confidence. Eventually, with their support, I became chair of the CGIT leadership committee for the entire Maritime region, something I never thought I'd be able to do.

I was in church from the cradle but didn't get baptized until I was an adult. My church was very hierarchical and patriarchal, and I wasn't really sure if I wanted to belong to it. But one of the older ladies in the church took me aside and told me that since I was leading a group of young women, I should put my money where my mouth is and lead by example.

I decided it was better to try and stay in something, and change it from within, as opposed to leaving and going somewhere else. And I couldn't really leave my church, because all of my family was there. My history was there.

"I WANT MORE FROM YOU"

I didn't really feel a call to ministry, but I was working in my church and I wanted to do more. I wanted to really *serve*, but the only way for me to serve at that time would have been as a deacon. And our minister had been known to say, "There'll be no women deacons in this church except over my dead body!"

I'd become a member of the Women's Inter-Church Council of Canada (WICC) and met women who introduced me to Christian feminist theology. I did a lot of reading and was introduced to feminist imagery in the Bible—like, you know, the picture of God as a mother hen. I came to realize that God could call women just as much as he could call men. That concept had never been part of my upbringing or teaching, so I explored that a bit.

I didn't get into everything I read. I'm not a radical. Like, some Christian feminists go as far as far as talking about "goddesses" and so on. That's not me. The basic thing I learned is that men and women are both called by God, and neither is above the other.

I moved further along in my work with the WICC. I was the North American representative at their quadrennial meetings, so I got to attend meetings in Australia and Jamaica, and work on services for the World Day of Prayer. A friend of mine, Jean Gordon, was instrumental in getting me involved with the WICC. She was the wife of a former Baptist pastor, and she gave me a lot of good advice. We once went to a conference in separate vehicles, and I drove past Jean and her husband on the highway. When we arrived at our destination, they came to my room to talk about my driving—because I had been speeding, it's true. So that's just the kind of person she was, and I learned a lot from her.

When people in the church told me I couldn't do something, I wanted to be able to refute that, so I decided I would try to find answers. I enrolled in a lay ministry course at the Atlantic School of Theology (AST) in Halifax. That program really interested me, and I wanted to learn more. Several of my professors at AST took me aside and suggested I pursue an MDiv. They saw something in me that I hadn't even sensed in myself.

In 1998, I graduated from AST with a diploma in lay ministry. Now I could respond when my minister and the deacons challenged me, so they agreed I could become a licentiate at the church—doing women's work.[1] I let them know I wasn't really interested in just being president of the ladies' auxiliary—I was hoping to do more.

There was another licentiate at the church during this time. He was given the opportunity to preach once a month on Sunday nights. They assigned him all the tasks a licentiate would normally do, while I was just ignored. Even *he* went to the deacons' board and said, "Hey, I do all these tasks—how come Sherrolyn doesn't get to do some of this?"

But we had a minister at Victoria Road who was in our church for fifty-one years. If he didn't like what you said in a church meeting, he'd pretend you hadn't said it. That happened to me and to the only other woman who would actually speak up and challenge him.

By this time, I *was* feeling a call to ministry. I couldn't identify it as such, and I still didn't know I was drawn to pastoring, but it was as if God was telling me, "I want more from you." It just happened to be that at this time I was also retiring from teaching. I booked a trip to Brazil for the fall after I retired. But all through the summer, I was tormented. God was saying, "You've finished one thing, but it's not enough. I want more." And I'd say, "No, I'm sorry, God, but I'm going to Brazil!"

Well, the upshot of it was that I lost my deposit on the trip to Brazil and I enrolled to do my MDiv at Acadia Divinity College.

A GRIM INTERNSHIP

I was really accepted at Acadia, and there were other women studying there too. The only negativity I ever found was from some of the male students who had grown up in those areas where they still weren't in favour of women in ministry. And they made that known. They thought women should be happy teaching Sunday school and that our greatest aspiration should be to the role of Sunday school superintendent.

1. A licentiate has a license to minister from a church or association, but is not yet ordained.

For me, that was quite interesting, because I was much older. To see young men with those attitudes was really disappointing.

As it happened, my church's pastor retired and a new minister came on. I don't remember this, but he tells me that during his first month, I asked for an interview with him. Apparently I went in and told him I wanted to study for the ministry—and that if he didn't like it, basically, I was going to do it anyway. I told him I'd like to play a part in the church.

Even though I can't recall that meeting, I can see myself doing that. Anyway, the new minister was very encouraging, but the former pastor still attended the church, and his deacons still aligned with him. Both the new minister and I were in for a bit of a struggle.

I was permitted to do my student internship at Victoria Road, but the chair of the internship committee was a deacon who didn't care for me. All the other internship students seemed to get glowing feedback reports from their churches, but I never did. The deacon's wife actually said to me, "Well, we don't want to build you up too much because then you wouldn't have any place to go."

In other words, when it came to my feedback reports, instead of giving me an "excellent," they might give me "good"; and instead of giving me "good," they'd give me "fair." It got so bad that my minister had to call the course professor and let him know there was a bias against me and my work at the church was much better than those reports would indicate.

So my internship was grim.

There were ministers on the examining council who I knew weren't in favour of women in ministry, and one of them gave me a rough time. I was more fortunate that way, though, than one of my friends—she went in knowing that three people were going to vote against her, no matter what she said or did. The examination was an ordeal, but I just prayed while I answered their questions, asking God to help me say the right thing and put the words in my mouth.

I passed unanimously and was ordained in 2003. In the African Association, ordination services are a big thing. Everybody dresses in their robes. My service was held at Victoria Road, and the church presented me with this lovely clergy gown. That service was really special to me because people came from all the little elements of my life. I asked the new pastor, who had been so supportive, to give the ordination message, and one of my dear CGIT friends came from Cape Breton. She read Scripture for me, along with one of my former teaching colleagues. Some friends from Acadia sang at the service, and my internship mentor did the prayer. So each part of the service involved *people* who were meaningful to me, and each part of the *service* was meaningful—especially when they all came up and laid hands.

NEVER TRY TO WORK IN YOUR HOME CHURCH

Our pastor left Victoria Road to take on a new position, and the church asked me to come on as interim. And I loved that church and its people, so I really felt that God was calling me to do this. Looking back in hindsight, they say you should never try to work in your home church.

When one of the deacons offered me a salary, I broke it down, and it amounted to twelve dollars an hour. Even the treasurer came forward and said, "No. There's no way you can pay that salary." No one else would have been paid so little. So I was able to start at a salary of twenty dollars an hour, for twenty hours a week. But of course, at Victoria Road, there's no way I could serve only twenty hours. I was being paid part time, but I was working full time.

A couple of older ladies at the church weren't happy with women in ministry. They both told me so, though one of them thought I was doing a good job. I think the people in the church knew me too well and I didn't get the respect I should've been given.

I probably should have demanded more respect—but the church was in financial difficulty, so I didn't demand the things I should have. Nobody thought to pay me for funerals or weddings, for example. I asked the church to form a little committee so we could sit down and talk about what would be appropriate, but nobody volunteered.

All this time, the former long-standing minister was still working in the church. He was still the go-to person, and he was kind of undermining me. So I had a problem there.

After three years, I still hadn't been inducted. The regional minister told the church, "She's been here all these years. You should induct her." So the church said they would, but by this point, the writing was on the wall. I knew there would be no sincerity in the things they'd be saying. I'd desperately wanted to be inducted during those three years, but no one even suggested it, so I just said no—not now.

I kept on for another year and a half, but they weren't happy with me. I did a questionnaire to try and find out how we could make things better, and I got a couple really nasty messages which were hurtful. I mean, they still hurt, all these many years later. So I realized it was time, and in 2007, I resigned.

I felt I had let myself down. I'd let the church down. And worse, I felt that I'd let God down.

SHE WAS TALKING ABOUT RACE

I went into a five-month depression. I think if things had lasted much longer, I would've needed treatment. I just felt worthless, like I had failed.

Part of the problem was that nobody really knew what was going on except my internship mentor, the late Rev. Tracey Grosse.[2] One of the things she said to me was, "Don't be bitter; don't get bitter." That stayed with me, because there was a such a tendency in me towards bitterness. But I kept heeding those words and I

2. Tracey Grosse was the first woman ordained by a church in the African United Baptist Association. She was ordained in 1996 and passed away in 2020. Her sister, Twila Grosse, was featured on an episode of the *Atlantic Baptist Stories* podcast as well as the *Called to Serve* podcast. The episode is available at https://acadiadiv.ca/acbas/oral-history-project and on Spotify and Apple Podcasts.

think I did escape the bitterness, partly because of her support and understanding.

So there I was, wanting to serve, but not knowing where or how, and feeling that I couldn't serve anyway because I wasn't good enough. A friend did tell me that my ministry really hadn't been as bad as I thought, but that's how I was feeling.

The next August, I went to convention and got talking with some pastor friends who were sitting around. One of them had been doing pulpit supply in Mahone Bay, Nova Scotia. And she said, "You ought to go and do pulpit supply for them. I'm going to give your name."

I said, "No—you know, please don't. I'm finished."

And she said, "Well, if you were finished, you wouldn't have enough interest to come to convention." So she gave them my name.

In September I got a call from the people in Mahone Bay asking if I would do pulpit supply. I said I would. Then at the end of September, they asked me if I'd stay until Christmas, and I said I would. Then they had their annual meeting in January and voted to call me on a permanent part-time basis, and I've been at Mahone Bay now for almost fifteen years.

It's been like night and day compared to Victoria Road, as far as reception from the congregation. And it's so different from an African church. Both the congregation and I had to learn to adjust to one another. Our organist, who comes from a Lutheran background, does her best, but it's funny because she's used to chants and slow, ponderous music—certainly nothing like spirituals.

Sometimes seniors, especially if they are in the early stages of dementia, will tell you the truth, the whole truth, and nothing but the truth. I went to visit one of the older ladies at Mahone Bay, and she was talking about race: "We weren't really sure, you know, that we wanted you to come." But then she reached out and patted my hand and said, "Now that you're here, we really like you."

MAHONE BAY UNITED BAPTIST CHURCH

My induction service at Mahone Bay—which happened in a timely fashion—was attended by many of the people from Victoria Road, as well as a lot of my Acadia family. Mahone Bay wasn't used to having anything very lavish, so they were just going to have some sandwiches for a reception. I said to the head of the ladies' aid, "You know, many of these people are coming from a long distance, and they will have a long distance to go home. It would be nice if we had a dinner."

Well, that lady turned white as a sheet. I found out later that she was quite upset by my asking to have a dinner. She told somebody, "We don't do that! We've never done that!"

Anyway, we had a dinner, and it went beautifully. A highlight of my ministry was seeing my former Black congregation out in the kitchen doing dishes with my present White congregation, and everyone getting along so well.

The people at Mahone Bay have been very supportive. I've made friends there—real friends. It's a very small church, mostly seniors, so I refer to them as the "junior seniors" and the "senior seniors." Sometimes I wonder if I'm there for palliative care, but then things pick up. We've had some losses in the past few years that really hurt the congregation, but on the other hand, we've had four new people come last year, and that's really lifted our spirits. We've got a thriving Bible study. So things are going fairly well.

We celebrate African Heritage Month every year. After the first couple years of doing it, I decided, "Well, I'm not going to shove this down their throats." Then the congregation came to me and asked, "Aren't we going to have an African Heritage service this year?" So it came from them—that was good.

We have a 103-year-old in our congregation who is still coming to church. She told me a year or two ago that she thought her church-going days were over. She was in an assisted living facility, but the owners of the facility sold it to make plain apartments. So her nephew was trying to find a nursing home for her, and she failed the nursing home test—she was too cognitively aware and physically healthy! When her nephew found out she didn't qualify, he said, "I would think being 103 years old would be qualification enough!"

But anyway, she went to live with him, and now she's coming to church. She's not using a walker or cane anymore; she just leans on her great-niece's arm, and it's a real boost to the congregation to see her there, worshipping with us.

GOD KNOWS WHAT HE'S DOING

In ministry, you can expect some hiccups, but God is always there. And there are people out there who are ready, willing, and able to give you a push and their support. You can believe that God knows what he's doing when he calls you.

While I was at Victoria Road, we had one elderly deacon who had to move into a nursing home. When I went to visit him, he said, "So you're the new minister?" I said yes, and he replied, "And you're a woman?" I said yes, and then he slapped his knee and cackled: "Well, I know the deacons don't like that!"

It was just so cute to hear him say that. But the thing that gave me the most joy was when one of the other deacons went to visit him and they were talking about me. And this elderly man said, "I just love it when the pastor comes, because she brings God with her."

That was such a testament! That's what I always try to do, and to think that he felt that way was one of the highlights of my ministry.

Sherrolyn Riley
Interviewed July 11, 2023

QUESTIONS FOR DISCUSSION AND REFLECTION

1. Sherrolyn describes an experience of depression and says, "If things had lasted much longer, I would've needed treatment." When has your mental health affected your work? Are you comfortable accessing mental health supports when needed?
2. One mentor advised Sherrolyn to avoid becoming bitter in the face of challenging circumstances. When do you feel a tendency towards bitterness? How can you avoid it?
3. Sherrolyn sacrificed a trip to Brazil in order to enroll in seminary. Have you ever felt God asking you to give up something? What happened?
4. Have you ever attended a church whose congregation was predominantly from a different racial or ethnic background than your own? What was that experience like?

9

Sandra Sutherland

Sandra was ordained in 2005 at West End Baptist Church in St. John's, Newfoundland. She later pastored at First Baptist Church in Moncton, New Brunswick, and today serves as a spiritual director. Sandra describes how her ministry identity slowly developed, from desiring to be a pastor's wife to becoming ordained herself. She also explains how she and her husband were able to manage being called to different ministries.

MY NAME IS SANDRA SUTHERLAND, but I go by Sandy. I was born in 1955 in Fredericton, New Brunswick.

Because of my dad's job, my family moved around New Brunswick a lot, and whenever we came to a new community, the first thing my parents did was find us a church. In one church, they had a tightly bonded group of friends, and all those adults became significant role models for me. One of my pastors even took some of us youth to the hospital with him when he made calls, and gave us opportunities to preach. When I look back on it, that was the beginning of me recognizing some of my gifts for ministry, and those opportunities awakened my spiritual passion.

I actually tried to avoid thinking about full-time ministry for as long as I could, and was planning to pursue a career in journalism. I liked to write and was figuring out how I could get paid for that. My marks were good and I had all kinds of ambition! Then one weekend, I went to a retreat at Camp Wildwood, in McKee's Mills, New Brunswick. That event was run by students from Atlantic Baptist College (ABC),[1] and over the weekend I really sensed God calling me to go to ABC when I graduated from high school. I was still only in grade eleven, but the call was so clear to me that I lay awake all night wrestling with it. When the sun came up in the morning, I finally said yes to God.

THERE WAS NO PASTOR FOR ME TO MARRY

Part of what I feared about going into ministry was that I might end up a very lonely single missionary in some isolated post in the world—because that's what I figured ministry looked like for women. I did not want that. During my years at ABC, I realized one of my desires was to become a pastor's wife. When I look back on that now, I realize that was the *other* role model I'd seen for women who loved and served the church. During my years at ABC, I felt affirmed in my leadership gifts, but I still wasn't interested in ministry for myself.

1. Now Crandall University.

I went down to Gordon College near Boston, as many of us did in those days. I was pursuing a BA in English, but just a couple months before graduation, I realized I wasn't cut out to be a journalist and had to rethink my future. So I went to the library one afternoon and spread three sheets of paper out in front of me. On one, I wrote down everything I loved to do. On the next, I wrote down everything I knew I *could* do. And on the third, I wrote down everything I *hoped* to do.

The pattern was unmistakable. My heart was for the church and for ministry. But I was stumped, because there still was no pastor for me to marry! I thought, "Lord, what do I do?"

The Lord helped me realize there was a way. Back at ABC, the director of student life had been Christine MacDormand.[2] Before she was ordained, she went from working at ABC to ministering in a local church as their director of Christian education. I think Chris probably forged the trail for a lot of us women because she just slid into that local church role and did ministry beautifully. I realized I could follow her example. So that was my call, and in 1977 I registered for a Master of Religious Education at Gordon-Conwell Theological Seminary.

I CHOSE TO STAY HOME

The first thing I did once I sensed God's clear calling was to speak with my parents. They were very affirming—and bless their hearts, they helped me out financially though the cost would be significant. I also checked things out with several role models, who were all very affirming.

My story is a little bit unique in that, although I felt called to ministry, that didn't mean pursuing ordination for me. That step didn't come until much later in my life. After graduating from Gordon-Conwell, I flirted with the idea of staying in the United States, but God made it clear to me that I was called back to the Maritimes. This is the world I know best, and this is where

2. Christine MacDormand was interviewed for *Called to Serve*. The episode is available at calledtoserve.ca and on Spotify and Apple Podcasts.

he wanted to use me in ministry. By his grace, I was called to be Minister of Christian Education at the Riverview Baptist Church in New Brunswick. That was a secondary staff position that didn't require ordination, and I served there from 1979 to 1982.

After that, I was called to teach a few Christian education courses back at ABC—and also to administer their student volunteer program (as all their students were required to do volunteer work in the church or community). I worked there for four years, and it was during that time I met my husband Gordon. The college used to send instructors like me out to do conference teaching, and Gordon showed up at one of my sessions on Christian education. I actually thought, "Oh my goodness, I can't believe that guy is so interested in Christian ed!" He never took his eyes off me!

Anyway, that was the beginning. After we were married, we packed up and moved to Wolfville so Gordon could study for pastoral ministry at Acadia. Meanwhile, I did part-time Christian education for Wolfville Baptist Church. Even though I was never a student at Acadia, I always felt bonded to that school.

In 1989, Gordon was called to Springhill Baptist Church in Springhill, Nova Scotia. We were already expecting our first child, a son, and our daughter arrived nineteen months later. I chose to stay home with them. We were in Springhill for six years, and during that time I got to be the pastor's wife I always wanted to be. I thoroughly enjoyed that! I did a lot of volunteer work at that church in partnership with Gordon. We led the youth group and Bible studies, and of course we had a lot of fun raising the kids.

But I couldn't just sit on my Christian ed training. I eventually got really restless at home, longing to be back on a church staff where I could make my contribution. My husband understood that, so when West End Baptist Church[3] in St. John's, Newfoundland, called asking if Gordon would be their lead pastor, *he* asked if they'd be interested in calling me too, to do Christian education. I think West End's motto in those days was, "We'll try anything once!" So in 2001, they hired us both.

3. Now The Crossing Church.

"IT'S TIME YOU LET THE CHURCH HOLD YOU ACCOUNTABLE"

In the beginning my hours were few at West End, but they continued to grow over time. During our ministry there, a beautiful, gracious Christian gentleman started coming alongside me saying, "Sandy, you need to think about being ordained." When he said that, I'd just laugh, but he was persistent. Finally one day, I agreed to begin praying about it.

When I brought it up before the Lord, I felt a growing sense within me that ordination was important and it was something he wanted me to do. I recognized I had a naive and unrealistic sense of what ordination meant. I was caught up in the title of becoming a "Reverend," afraid it would put a wedge between me and laypeople, and fearing it would somehow negate the ministry I'd already done. I know that doesn't really make sense, but that's what I was dealing with at the time.

One day, another pastoral friend called my husband at the church. I answered the phone and took a moment to chat with this much-respected Christian leader. I told him, "I think I'm being called to be ordained." And he said, "Well, it's about time." That kind of shocked me, but he went on and said, "It's time you had the church affirm your ministry and your gifts. And it's time you let the church hold you accountable for your ministry."

That really shocked sense into me, so I said, "Lord, if this is what you want, please make it clear in these three conversations." Because of course, I knew I had to talk to my husband first, and then our children, and I also wanted to check it out with my mom and dad.

My husband was marvellous about it. He's always been 100 percent supportive. I marvel at him in so many ways, because it might be hard to move over and make room for a wife in pastoral ministry, but he's *never* withheld his support. And when I talked with our teenage kids, they said with a smile, "Well, Mom, we're already PKs.[4] How much worse can it get?" I loved that answer.

4. Pastor's kids.

When I called my parents, my dad was quietly supportive, and my mom said, "I've always felt you should have the title 'Reverend.'" I couldn't have asked for more encouragement and affirmation.

ORDINATION AT WEST END BAPTIST CHURCH

I didn't have to do an internship for ordination because of my cumulative years of ministry. But I did have to write my statement of faith, which was a tremendous learning exercise. Then in 2005 I met with the examining council. Many of my good friends and colleagues were present on that council, and I felt greatly encouraged by their affirmation of my call to ministry. My husband was even on council at the time—they wouldn't let him participate, of course, but he got to escort me into the room, which pleased everybody.

West End blessed me with a beautiful ordination service. I was nervous and had my own self-conscious issues to manage, but it ran very smoothly and was quite celebratory! I invited Chris MacDormand to be one of my speakers, and also asked a couple of my girlfriends from the mainland to read Scripture and pray during the service. Because of my ministry in Christian education, I was serving four generations of people. Sometimes we think Christian ed is just about children and youth, but it's actually the teaching ministry for adults as well. So I asked a representative from each of those four generations if they would let me wash their feet during the service. They really didn't want to, but they did it for me out of love!

I realized almost immediately after my ordination that that little title of "Reverend" rarely gets used in daily life. What *really* happened for me during that process was that I sensed a new power in my ministry, and a greater freedom to be who God was calling me to be as a pastor. It was less about me and more about the Holy Spirit within me—less about me struggling and striving within myself, because I had a greater freedom to lean into God and let God use me.

Sandra Sutherland

"WE'LL FIND A WAY"

We were in St. John's, Newfoundland, for thirteen years. My role kept changing, and by the end of our ministry I was the children's pastor. Meanwhile, Gordon had been working on his doctorate, and his thesis was on intentional interim ministry. When we finished at West End and came back to the mainland, that's the kind of work he began doing. Then I thought, "Well, what about me, Lord? We're breaking up the team here. What do I do?"

I wondered if it was time for me to shift out of pastoral ministry and try my hand at something new. I went away on a retreat and spent a few days with a spiritual director. By the end of that, I sensed clearly that God wasn't finished with me in pastoral ministry yet. But I had no idea what that could look like or how Gordon and I would pull it off, because he was going to have to move from church to church in the work he was doing.

Right after the retreat ended, Gordon picked me up and took me out for lunch. I shared with him what God had put on my heart, and then we went back to work. There in my office, on my computer, was an invitation to apply to be the associate pastor for First Baptist Moncton in New Brunswick. That was the exact timing of my receiving it. And when I read the job description, I shut my computer down and thought, "Oh, Lord, that's too much for me."

But when I opened it again and read more carefully, I realized the role had all the things I wanted to be able to do in ministry. I ran down the hallway to my husband's office, in tears because I didn't know how we could manage it. But Gordon said, "We'll find a way." And we did.

I was at First Baptist Moncton for six years, from 2014 to 2020. During that time, Gordon served at four other churches, and some of them were a long distance away. But we did some specific things to make it work. For example, we asked each of our churches for one weekend off a month so we could be with the other in their congregation. Gordon was my first phone call every morning and my last call every night, and he came home for at least one day every week.

Sometimes we pastors are afraid to ask our churches for what we need. But the older I get, the more I am an advocate for our self-care in ministry. And that includes being able to nurture our marriages, if we are married. We have to negotiate very honestly with our spouses and churches about what we need to protect our marriages, and to help them grow stronger and flourish in the midst of challenging circumstances.

There's no way Gordon and I could've made our ministries work without God's help. The two callings—both mine and my spouse's—were clearly from the Lord. I laugh now when I look back. There I was, a young woman, longing to be a pastor's wife. Look at where that part of my life carried me! When I showed up in the churches Gordon was serving, they *only* knew me as his wife, and I loved that role. As a pastor's wife, the best thing you can do is simply love the people. That's all you have to do—and they love you back. There's nothing like it.

SHE SIMPLY HAD HER EYES ON THE LORD

God gave me wonderful opportunities at First Baptist Moncton that I'd never had before. I got to preach more, and began to conduct funerals. I did pastoral care with seniors. And one of my favourite things—which I'd never done before because I was afraid to do it—was that I got to baptize people. I stayed at that church until I officially retired at sixty-five years old.

Recently, I've been able to pursue a couple of other things God started growing in my heart during my time as a pastor. For example, we had a pretty terrific experience with our children's ministry in Newfoundland. I always felt that God wanted me to write that up in a book, so after I retired that's what I did.[5]

The second thing I felt drawn to was the ministry of spiritual direction. During my time in Moncton, I got to know Cheryl Ann

5. Sandra Sutherland, *Children on the Trail: A Child's Spiritual Formation Guide for Churches and Parents* (Winnipeg: Word Alive, 2022).

Beals, the director of CBAC's Sozo Centre for Soul Care. I never dreamed of being able to work with her, but while I was enrolled in a training program for spiritual directors, she invited me onto her team. I've been doing spiritual direction ever since—I love being able to minister one-on-one to people.

I don't know if I've ever been able to sort out the joys and challenges specific to being a woman in ministry. One thing I loved was the opportunity to work on teams where both men and women were using their gifts. That experience makes me think of completion, and enrichment, and having greater depth and scope.

I think the challenges in my ministry were less to do with being a woman and more to do with being in secondary staff positions. Those positions come with their own unique challenges, and because of my own broken personality and the ways I've dealt with some things insensitively or immaturely, I've had to learn some hard lessons.

Even though I often feel upset when I have conversations with people who are against women in ministry, I also have understanding and compassion towards them. Maybe because it was a journey for *me*, and I had to follow the Lord through a transition in my theology. I realize that a lot of what the apostle Paul writes about women in the church is confusing, so I try to remember it confused me for a long time, too. I realize not everybody has had the privilege of studying those Scriptures the way I have.

I was once asked to write an article about women in ministry and I chose to research Rev. Josephine Moore. She was ordained in 1954, and the more I got to know her, the more I could relate. She married one of the deacons in her church, so she was a pastor and a wife. They had two children like we did, so she was also a mother. She was gentle and humble and devoted to the Lord. God blessed her ministry, and he's still blessing it—if someone like me, all this time later, thinks about her example, then God is still using her! And here's the thing: she was never aggressive about being a woman in ministry. She simply had her eyes on the Lord.

I read a testimony from her daughter that said Rev. Moore's heart just longed to do what God wanted her to—honoring and glorifying the Lord was her passion. You can't argue with that in someone's ministry. No matter what you think about women in ministry, you just can't argue with that!

CALLED TO STEP UP

Looking back on my own ministry, I think I probably used the fact that I was a woman to escape greater responsibility. I would hold back and let myself think it was OK—because I was a woman, I didn't *need* to step up. Basically, I was just afraid to grow and stretch and take on more responsibility. But at some point in my journey towards ordination, the Lord showed me Gal 3:26–28 in an entirely new way. I'd always read those verses thinking they were calling us to unity, which they are. They say: "So in Christ Jesus you are all children of God through faith, for all of you who were baptized into Christ have clothed yourselves with Christ. There is neither Jew nor Gentile, neither slave nor free, nor is there male and female, for you are all one in Christ Jesus."[6]

At that critical point in my experience with God, I saw that everything is usurped by the presence and power of the Holy Spirit in our lives. I saw every difference we have disappear in the powerful unity of the Holy Spirit. And then God spoke to me and said, "If you, like all these others in Christ, have the Holy Spirit within you, then you have gifts of the Holy Spirit that need to be used. The church needs those. And I'm calling you to step up and use them."

I recognized my responsibility—that I couldn't hide behind being a woman. I couldn't *not* step out and take risks, and step into new opportunities to use my gifts. I'm an introvert. It was always hard for me; it still is. But only with God's enabling, with the courage and help he gives me by his Holy Spirit, am I able to step up and step out in ministry.

Sandra Sutherland
Interviewed July 11, 2023

6. NIV.

QUESTIONS FOR DISCUSSION AND REFLECTION

1. One of Sandra's pastors gave her opportunities to minister from a young age. Are there age restrictions on how young people can serve in your church? How can churches intentionally help children and teenagers explore the ways they are gifted?
2. Encouragement from male colleagues was essential in affirming Sandra's call to ministry. How can male leaders uniquely support women and make space for them to step into their callings?
3. Sandra admits that she avoided the idea of full-time ministry because she feared becoming a "lonely single missionary in some isolated post." What assumptions do you have about what it means for someone to be in ministry?
4. Sandra and her husband were both called to ministry, sometimes in a team dynamic and other times at different churches. If you're married, how can you support your spouse to use their strengths and gifts? What kinds of support might a pastor's family need from their church?

10

Marion Jamer

Marion was ordained in 2011 and has served as a pastor and a community chaplain in Nova Scotia, working alongside first responders. In this chapter, she shares stories of supporting the RCMP and fire department, describing her ministry as that of an evangelist. She notes the advantage she had as a chaplain because she worked together with those she served.

Marion Jamer

My name is Marion Jamer. I was born in St. Charles, Illinois, in 1955.

My mom and dad met at Wheaton College, and they attended a non-denominational college church. I have relatives in denominations ranging from Fellowship Baptist, to Lutheran, to Plymouth Brethren, to Salvation Army. There's a long history in my family of pastors and preachers. My great-grandfather was H. A. Ironside, who was a prolific writer, fundamentalist, and dispensationalist. He travelled around the United States and Great Britain preaching—although I don't always agree with his theology. And every generation after him was a pastor: my grandfather and my father. But I'm the first female pastor in the family that I'm aware of.

When I was less than two years old, I was in a severe car accident and my face was smashed quite badly. So I had reconstructive surgery around my mouth and nose, under a local anaesthetic. This left me with trauma and panic attacks that would come whenever I'd hear a siren, although I always chased fire trucks.

When I was two, we moved to New Brunswick. I remember going to church when I was a very little girl, and then "playing church," standing in front of an imaginary congregation and leading the responsive reading. I can remember trying to evangelize in elementary school by writing Bible verses in the snow and through other kinds of childish (or childlike) ways of trying to share the good news, which I really and truly believed in.

My father was a school principal, but he was also a pastor who filled in for a variety of churches in Carleton County. So sometimes I'd go visit churches with him, but usually we'd attend the Baptist church in Florenceville, New Brunswick. My mom was always very active in ministry with my dad, informally, as a pastor's wife. Although she was one of the most capable Bible teachers around, she would not teach an adult Sunday school class if men were in attendance. She would have grown up with the idea that women didn't even speak in church.

Camp Shiktehawk played a major role in my spiritual formation. I was sixteen when I really began to take discipleship seriously, in a more mature way. I remember coming home from camp one week and my parents asking, "What happened to you?" I don't know what we call it as Baptists, but it was some kind of filling of the Holy Spirit. My sister and I were both baptized—which, because we didn't come from strictly Baptist roots, wasn't something we talked a lot about. It was a very serious decision for me to make.

I was really active in my church. I did all the leadership roles that were available: teaching Sunday school, camp counselling, and serving as president of the Baptist youth association in our area. One of the books on my shelf was called *How to Be a People Helper*. And I think, really, I have always felt a call to ministry. It just grew stronger and stronger.

"IF I CAN'T BECOME A PASTOR . . ."

Around sixteen or seventeen, I began to notice that it was much easier for a young man to say he was going into ministry. I remember one incident in which myself and a guy were being considered for a position, and he was given the position even though he wasn't really active in the church—I think because he was male. It began to make me question: just how am I going to do this? I might as well have been expecting to be an astronaut or something. So when it came to my high school yearbook and answering the question of what I wanted to do, I skirted the issue of ministry. I didn't want to put it in there because I wasn't sure how it could work out.

Of course, this was just around the turn of the decade with the 1970s. There was a lot happening in the world, but it wasn't happening in Baptist churches.

I went to the Atlantic Baptist College[1] in Moncton and left after a year, then went down to Gordon College in Massachusetts and again left after part of a year. I wasn't really going where I wanted to go and so I dropped out of university. Then I married my husband, and he's also a pastor. So I became the quintessential pastor's wife—the safe place for women in ministry at the time!

1. Now Crandall University.

My husband was going to Ontario Bible College, and I was supportive of him doing that. So I gave up my educational aspirations, and it wasn't until I had my third child that I went back to university at UNB.[2]

It was a really tough decision to go back to school. They didn't have distance education and things like you do now. My children were in grade one and kindergarten, and the youngest was about a year old. I thought, "I'll do a BA in English. I can read books while I'm doing things with children. And it will also help me if I'm teaching Sunday school or doing Bible studies or things like that—learning to work with literature will be a useful skill." That was always in the back of my mind, but I thought, "If I can't become a pastor, then I will go into the education system and become a teacher."

I ended up working as a substitute teacher for thirteen years. Then I was looking for some way to get a master's degree, so I found a little loophole in the Master of Education program at UNB, and that was to do critical studies. I ended up with half my courses in curriculum and instruction, and the other half in adult education. Which, again, I was thinking: *Adult education—that's a great thing to use in the church.* I was always keeping ministry in mind.

ROLE MODELS WERE HARD TO FIND

In 2005 we moved down to Hantsport, Nova Scotia, about twenty minutes away from Acadia Divinity College (ADC). By this time, my children had mostly left home, so I was trying to figure out how to explain to my husband that I was once again going back to school. He always rolls his eyes when I say that.

One of the women in our church paid for my first course. Another woman was *very* kind: she got a diagnosis that she was terminally ill with cancer, and she knew that I needed a vehicle to travel. She said, "I know you have been working with the youth group. If you want, I'll sell you my van for a dollar when I die."

2. University of New Brunswick.

And so, with God's provision, I started on my MDiv. It took me a very long time. I was thinking, "I might be able to graduate in time to retire!"

It wasn't until my time at ADC that I really knew any female pastors or chaplains. I saw women doing ministry before that, but the problem was they weren't given formal recognition. For example, I saw that youth pastors were males who had full-time positions, but if you were female, you were called "coordinator" or something like that. And almost without exception, if women had a job, it was with children's ministry or women's ministry. Role models among senior leadership were really hard to find. When I began to study church history, I realized how involved women have been in ministry, in so many contexts. Repeatedly, they would gain a certain level of prominence in the church, and then it would just seem to disappear. It was comforting to know that historical women struggled with a lot of the same obstacles.

While I was doing my studies, I still had one child at home and my husband was in full-time ministry. I was working part-time as well as volunteering as a chaplain. So it was incredibly busy. I had a wonderful colour-coded calendar, so I knew exactly how much time I had to do whatever needed to be done. I made sure that I had time to spend with my husband and my kids. We made it a habit that, if we didn't do anything else, we'd have at least one meal each day when we sat down together.

My family got pulled into my seminary world. My husband loves to cook, so we'd invite students over so he could get to know them, and our teenage son became friends with some of the students as we played games. As a family, we intertwined a lot of the stuff we did with the school. I did gain a bit of a reputation for sometimes lingering in the hallway and being a little late to class—but I think sometimes you have to prioritize people and make sure you're doing the important things.

FIREFIGHTER TRAINING

I graduated with my MDiv in 2010, in the youth pastor track. I love working with young people and young adults. Doing the practicum part of my degree was a little awkward, because I didn't want to work in my home church with my pastor, who was my husband. But God had graciously brought us somewhere where there were two retired pastors. They had areas of specialty that intrigued me—one had worked with addictions counselling, and the other had served in the Navy and was a fire chaplain in Hantsport. And so things began to align, and as part of my ministry practicum it was suggested I join the fire department as a chaplain.

For me, to think about being with the fire department was quite a step, because it meant overcoming the trauma I'd had in my personal life. When I went to the first meeting, I remember how strange it smelled in the truck bay. I walked in and looked at all these people and thought, "Oh my. What am I getting into?"

But I had come to the conclusion that the only way for me to really be a good chaplain for the firefighters was to understand their work. And I saw the fire department as a really good place to connect with our community overall. I knew that, as a family, we would continue to move when my husband was called to pastor different churches. So I thought, "If I can connect with fire departments, it will give me a way into every new community we go to."

I asked the Hantsport fire chief if I could take level one firefighter training, and he said, "Oh, sure." So I signed up and arrived the first night. There were three or four of us there for training. The others kind of looked around, and the chief hemmed and hawed, and then he said to me, "So, you're driving the light rescue truck tonight, because none of the others are old enough to be insured to drive it."

I thought, "Oh, no—this is going to be interesting." The light rescue is larger than a pickup truck, with a big box on the end. I had a bunch of young guys sitting in the back, trying to put their safety in the hands of a woman who'd never driven that vehicle before. And I'm sure the training instructor looked at me and thought I was a most unlikely candidate. I would have agreed.

But as I began to do the training and get involved, I discovered I really enjoyed being a firefighter. Now, I couldn't do everything the young people could do—and I thought it would have been a whole lot easier to do about thirty years before. However, I got more involved, to the point that within a year, I started responding to every call and taking an active role. I did everything from traffic control to being the safety officer and the accountability officer, making sure we know where everybody is on scene. There's a lot of responsibility with the role, but I grew to really love it.

THEY CRY OUT TO TWO PEOPLE: GOD AND THEIR MOTHER

I found there was less resistance to me being a woman in ministry in the community than there was in churches. I've always enjoyed sports and enjoyed doing things that were sometimes considered more male-dominated, so I felt quite comfortable in the fire department setting. A couple of my mentors wondered how I would survive there, with the language and the culture, and I said, "No, I think I'm OK with that!" I remember the first time one of the firefighters dropped the F-bomb in my presence, and he kind of looked at me, and we just kept on going. It was like, as far as I'm concerned, I just want you to do your job. I'm not here to judge.

So it hasn't been an issue in terms of harassment or non-acceptance. In some ways, I think being female has been an advantage for me. One of my mentors said, "When soldiers are in danger, they cry out to two people: God and their mother." And I think because I came in as an older woman, there wasn't some of the tension there might have been with a younger female. Like, I'm not trying to do their job. I do the roles I can, but I'm not in competition, and I think a lot of them have appreciated that.

I really think my gender has been more advantage than disadvantage. Although, the first fire I went to, I was on the scene in bunker gear for eleven hours with no washroom. The men have a distinct advantage there! So women tend not to hydrate as much as men do on scenes—it's like, "OK, we'll wait!"

I really decided I would take on that firefighting culture and become part of it, and I think that's one of the reasons I've been so accepted. The first funeral I had was a fire department funeral. It was one of our drivers, who had been really kind to me. He had gone out on a call the day before, and I remember hearing the pager go off. He'd had a cardiac arrest. That funeral was complicated, but my husband came to support me—he was sweating bullets and hoping I didn't totally mess up.

I also began working as a chaplain with the RCMP. They're a very difficult group to break into; they're very closed and suspicious. And one of the advantages for me as a chaplain was, because I did the firefighter training, I was able to go on scenes. I've been on scenes with them when they're going through things, and so when I go into the RCMP detachments, they know I understand. I've been out on those calls. I've seen them in action. It's meant I'm actually part of what they're doing and not just somebody coming in.

You can see the difference with chaplains who have a little bit more of an arm's length distance from the people they're serving. I don't think everybody has to join the fire service or whatever, but I think it was a distinct advantage that I was willing to do that.

I'VE ORDAINED YOU TO BEAR MUCH FRUIT

I was ordained in 2011. One of the gifts I received was a paintball gun, because I love playing paintball. And I was so delighted when I had a whole row of firefighters from my department come to the ordination service. They came into the church and looked so sheepish, not knowing what to do, but they were all there. There were a few comments about them being afraid the roof was going to cave in, but it didn't, and we were good!

I knew when I was preparing for the examining council that there were people who'd had very negative experiences there. So when I was crafting my statement of faith, I was careful. I will admit to putting in a few red herrings that I hoped some people would chase, instead of asking some of the questions I didn't really want to answer.

My theology has changed a bit over time. Particularly, as I moved into chaplaincy, I realized I was less of a theologian and more of an evangelist. I came across the distinction in some of the reading I was doing: a theologian is convinced that you have to understand and have a distinct position, but as an evangelist in a chaplain's role, you have to be open to other people's ideas and positions. Although you hold your own views, you hold them a little more lightly than some people, and a little quieter in some ways. If I'm working with you as a chaplain, it doesn't matter as much what *I* believe. It's more: how can I guide you in *your* journey of faith without imposing mine on you?

I think my degree in English and the education degree in critical studies have made me less dogmatic. I do think there is such a thing as real, definable truth, but I think sometimes we have different perspectives that can *look* like we hold different truths.

I'm pretty orthodox. I'm relatively conservative, but not as conservative as some Baptists. Over the course of my ministry, the Southern Baptist Convention in the United States has hotly debated women's ordination. I knew that, as a woman, I wouldn't even be allowed to be a chaplain there. And I know that here in Atlantic Canada, we have some people who follow closely what's going on in the SBC and align themselves. So people would ask me, "What if you encounter this? What if something happens?"

I'd had an experience while reading Scripture. I came to John 15:16, where Jesus says, "You did not choose me, but I chose you, and I've ordained you to bear much fruit. Because I've done this, you can ask what you will in my name and I'll give it to you."[3] And I remember looking out the picture window in my home in Hantsport and thinking, "What do I really want? If I can have anything, what do I want?" And I remember thinking, "I want people to come to know Jesus. I want to have an impact on people that helps them get to know God."

3. Paraphrased.

And so for me, there was a sense that although ordination would be important for me to have as a chaplain, I wasn't going to be ordained by men. It would be God who ordained me.

OUR POSITION IS TENUOUS

I have had a few ministry roles in churches. In Hantsport, I led services with my husband and worked with our youth group and a small group. They recognized they couldn't pay me there, so I had a conversation with them about whether they could give me a title, and they gave me the title of Community Chaplain. Then since moving to St. Stephen, New Brunswick, in 2014, I've been preaching at a very small country church. They wanted an ordained pastor to come do communion occasionally, with lay speakers preaching the rest of the time. It ended up being me preaching every week, so that's what I've been up to lately. But chaplaincy is what I love to do.

Things have changed when it comes to women in ministry, but sometimes not as much as we would like. During my time at ADC, I'd still have fellow students come up and tell me that they really thought women shouldn't be in ministry—to my face, they'd tell me that. I think women have to decide they're really called to something, and that became my answer: "I understand that you don't think this is scriptural, but I have to do what God tells me to do. I can't *not* obey."

We've had conversations at convention and Oasis over the years about women in ministry. It's been back and forth, and it depends on which group speaks at the microphone the most. A lot of the time, it's been like, "Well, let's not ruffle feathers with either the ones who feel really strongly or the ones who feel negatively that women should be there." Personally, because I come from the background I did, I have heard the arguments against women in ministry. I know and love people who hold that position. And the arguments aren't worth it.

I attended Oasis when Renée MacVicar[4] was being proposed for executive minister. It was very apparent that there were divergent views. And I can tell you, from my perspective on the floor and the conversations I had, many of us who were ordained women were afraid of how that would go. There were hurtful things being said. Sometimes we have felt like people have not stood up enough on our behalf, and again, given what's been happening in the Southern Baptist Convention, I think many of us are aware that our position is tenuous. It has been taken away from women in other places.

Feminism is not just one distinct idea. It's a whole series of ideas and a widely disputed thing. There are different waves of feminism. I think the closest I personally come to it is the idea of intersectionality, which means there are many things that make up your experience. It's not just whether you're male or female, woman or man, but it's also your race and socioeconomic status and all other kinds of things that contribute to your experience. When it comes right down to it, I think feminism is a secular response that is trying to right injustice, but I don't think they have it quite right. I think we need more spiritual understanding and wisdom when we're talking about these issues. Probably in a lot of people's books, I am a dyed-in-the-wool feminist, but I'm like, "No, no . . ."

I really take my stance from Scripture. I understand there are passages that talk about the role of women, but those must be understood in the context of their time. We are in a different place now, and ordination itself is far different—I don't think any of the disciples were "ordained" in the sense we mean. When Mary was sent out to tell the disciples that Christ was risen, *she* was ordained—maybe in the same way I always felt I was, which is being given a task by God to do something.

4. Renée MacVicar was interviewed for *Called to Serve*. The episode is available at calledtoserve.ca and on Spotify and Apple Podcasts.

GOOD SAMARITANS

I went right from my MDiv to my DMin program. I wanted to focus on preparing chaplains to work with firefighters and other first responders who have repeated exposure to trauma. That proved to be a really fruitful thing, and I graduated with that in 2018.

It has been incredibly rewarding to work with first responders as a chaplain. They are really good people. One of the guiding stories in my life is the story of the Good Samaritan. The religious people leave the man by the side of the road, and it's the unlikely person who rescues him. And I sometimes say, you know, sometimes angels show up in bunker gear or police uniforms. We need to be aware of the challenges they face.

There's a lot more faith in the community than we sometimes stereotypically think, and people are more open if you can speak their language. I hope as people in our churches begin to understand that, there's an openness—to not be quite so judgemental, and not be like, "Nobody's going to church anymore!" Sometimes we have to go out and find people. And I think that's the evangelist in me: let me meet you on your turf, and let's have those conversations.

And I've had some really good ones. I've seen spiritual growth in RCMP members that has blown my mind. Now, other times, it seems like I'm not getting anywhere. But let your light shine, and people will ask. They'll want to know. Don't be afraid of stepping outside your comfort zone—for me, that's been incredibly rewarding.

When I first started riding in the back of a fire truck, I would literally laugh. It was like, "God, what are you doing? I can't believe I'm actually doing this." But people are really in need of spiritual care, and some of them don't know where to find it. And I think we can provide it in so many ways. Yesterday I set out on a walk, not knowing where I was going or who I'd meet, but praying as I went, and it was just perfect timing to have conversations with three different people.

So be a little daring. Look for those openings. Find those spots and just let God direct your steps. There's so many divine appointments that I have every day, and I'm completely convinced God can arrange those times for us. So, I'm totally optimistic about the church and totally optimistic about where God is going right now. And I think that sense of hope is something we need to share.

Marion Jamer
Interviewed February 10, 2024

QUESTIONS FOR DISCUSSION AND REFLECTION

1. As a teenager, Marion noticed that it was easier for young men to go into ministry than it was for young women. Do you think this is still true today?
2. Marion writes, "There was less resistance to me being a woman in ministry in the community than there was in churches." Have you found that women are treated differently in church compared to the community?
3. Marion was surprised that she ended up doing ministry by riding in the back of a fire truck. When has God surprised you in your life?
4. What challenges do first responders face in your community? How can Christians minister to those who work in vital community services?

11

Louise Hannem

Louise was ordained in 2012 at Bayers Road Baptist Church in Halifax, Nova Scotia. She pastored in several churches before taking on a full-time role with Canadian Baptist Ministries, where her work focuses on global mission and justice issues. In this chapter, Louise describes the unique challenges of taking maternity leave as a pastor and how she tries to maintain balance as a single parent.

My name is Louise Hannem, and I was born in 1982 in Halifax, Nova Scotia.

Growing up in a church family, my experience was mostly positive. We attended a traditional Baptist church on Sundays, and in my memory, that meant sitting still and quietly drawing on the back of offering envelopes with those tiny pew pencils. If you got a sharp one, it was a bonus day, because they usually weren't sharp and there was no way to sharpen them, either!

Other than those quiet services of serene tradition, I remember church was also a place of joy and laughter. I was part of midweek programs and youth group and summer camp, and I also confess that I was part of a puppet ministry. That was in the nineties, and I wish I could say it was cool then, but I don't think it was.

I enjoyed being part of my church community, and it was certainly a place where I felt like I belonged. I had friends there, but there were also older adults who cared about me, and that was really significant. One influential leader in my life was Michele Bland. She currently serves as a lead pastor for a church in Hong Kong, but she was a youth pastor at my home church in Halifax for a couple of years.[1] She had a profound impact on me. She was so vibrant and cool and so much fun. She was a great teacher, and she loved to laugh—she's so funny. She really shared her life with us.

My grandmother was also a significant role model for me. She was so tenacious—feisty, actually, is a better word. She was loyal and committed, and so articulate. She had a deep passion for mission and served in leadership roles in many ways, and she loved people really deeply. Most importantly, she was the one who taught me how to pray. I think if she had been born in a different era, she absolutely would have been a phenomenal pastor.

Growing up in the church wasn't a perfect experience. Looking back now as an adult, I recognize some unhelpful theological messages were communicated. But that's just part of growing and learning, and being part of a community that's trying to learn together.

1. Michele Bland was interviewed for *Called to Serve*. The episode is available at calledtoserve.ca and on Spotify and Apple Podcasts.

Louise Hannem

THE LEVITICAL CALL

While I was in university, I worked as a summer student intern at my home church, Bayers Road Baptist in Halifax. I also worked at two different summer camps, and for Atlantic Baptist Women doing children's ministries. Then in 2006, I started working full-time at Bayers Road. It was initially to cover a maternity leave for our director of Christian education, but then nine years later, I was still there.

I don't know if I had a specific moment when I heard "the call," but there was a specific moment when I learned how God had been calling me all along. That was during a day for prospective students at Acadia Divinity College (ADC). I think it was actually the third time I went to that event, because each year somebody suggested I should go, and someone else would drive me there. I didn't protest because there was always a free lunch that tasted really good. It was also good to be surrounded by great thinkers and meet interesting people.

At one of those events, Dr. Glenn Wooden was presenting about God's calling on our lives and describing some of the ways that happens. Before his session, I had really only been familiar with the idea of God's call being like the call of Moses—you know, sort of a "burning bush" experience. And because I hadn't had *that* experience in my life, I assumed I wasn't called to a significant leadership role in the church. And that was actually fine with me; I was OK with not having that call.

But the burning bush was only one of many types of calling experiences that Dr. Wooden went over that day. And he presented these various calls so carefully and pastorally. I remember him walking us through the "Levitical call." He said something like, "These are the people who have been raised in the temple to do God's work, and they don't know anything else. It's just really natural to them." Hearing him say *that* was like an audible "burning bush" voice for me. It seemed that those words were meant for me in that moment, and that was really comforting but also terrifying.

Ministry was all I had known. It was all I was passionate about, and it was the place where I felt at home. It was probably like if you were raised on a farm your whole life and then you announced you were going to be a farmer, no one would be shocked. My call wasn't earth-shattering for anyone. But it was a significant moment for me to understand that God calls us in different ways, and no call is more significant than another. That clarity was helpful going forward.

YOU'RE THERE TO SAY "GOD"

I was already working full-time at my church and had started taking a few courses at ADC, so I began doing what's called a Certificate in Christian Studies. I thought, "Maybe I'll just do one year. I'll get a certificate and that should be OK." But very quickly, I realized that wasn't going to work, and I started slowly picking away at an MDiv.

I felt very supported at ADC. I can't think of a time when there was any conflict around being a woman. Everyone there was not only supportive and encouraging, but also a real advocate for women in ministry.

I underwent the process of ordination with the examining council in 2012, going before them in the very early days of my maternity leave. I strolled into my interview on maybe four hours of sleep and had a stroller with me, carrying my six-week-old baby. I could hear her crying in the room next to us during my interview—she was with my mom, who was helping me that day.

The moderator for my interview was Harry Gardner, and he was so pastoral and supportive. The room was full, which was a bit intimidating, although I think I was too sleep-deprived to really register any of that. My senior pastor attended the interview as a guest, and he counted over forty questions that were asked during those sixty minutes of my interview. So it was fast. But it didn't feel rushed—I felt questioned and not interrogated. I had time to answer the questions about my statement of faith and also to share more personally about my passions, like my interest in global mission and justice issues.

I received a unanimous vote, and so I was ordained at Bayers Road. Two years later, I transitioned from my role as their director of Christian education to being associate pastor at Timberlea Baptist Church in Timberlea, Nova Scotia. I pastored there until 2019. In all, I served for around twelve years in local church pastoral ministry.

I learned so much as a pastor, and people were so gracious to me. I learned how to preach and lead communion and baptize people and visit in the hospital, and how to lead a youth ministry—renting vans and getting permission forms and making sure the right number of kids were in the seats. I learned how to run a retreat, and how to sit with people in their pain, and how to conduct funeral services, and lead a wedding and dedicate a baby and celebrate all those really significant moments in people's lives—those moments when, as Eugene Peterson says, you're there to say "God."[2] Pastoral ministry was an honour.

CANADIAN BAPTIST MINISTRIES

While I was pastoring, I worked in a small contract role for Canadian Baptist Ministries (CBM). So in 2019, I transitioned to working on CBM's Church Engagement Team. I've been there full-time since then. What we do is invite Canadian churches to join with the church in the majority world[3] and partner in meaningful ways—not just financially, but also in learning about their context, learning from our global brothers and sisters, being prayer partners, and visiting if appropriate.

Part of my job is speaking at many churches and creating resources for them. I also oversee SENT, CBM's short-term mission program. We send teams from our various Canadian Baptist denominations—whether it's a team of youth or university students,

2. Eugene H. Peterson and Calvin Miller, *Weddings, Funerals, and Special Events* (Carol Stream, IL: Word Books, 1987), 16.

3. Africa, Asia, and Latin America.

or a gap-year program, or a women's group or church-based team. We send this variety of teams cross-culturally to visit our partners around the world.

At CBM, we work only through partnerships, and so we work only in places where we've been invited to come and partner. We always look for partners who are like-minded in significant ways, but we also recognize there's so much beauty in diversity. We have partners who would land in different spots on some theological issues, for sure. At times we're in settings where there aren't ordained women in leadership. But we believe we are richer together in our diversity, and in humility we are able to work alongside each other and put aside those differences for the kingdom. There is a deep commitment to partnership in our work, understanding that mutuality in partnership doesn't mean we're all the same or that we agree on everything, but that we're committed to the things that are most significant.

In our work, that's joining God in what he's doing around the world: caring for the poor and the marginalized, caring for kids at risk, working for justice, and building the church. All of those things are really core to who we are.

TAKING MATERNITY LEAVE AS A PASTOR

I was involved in ministry long before I had kids. It was just a part of life. And so it certainly was a big adjustment to add kids into it—especially pastoral ministry, when you're working a lot of evenings. And obviously weekends are always a time of work.

I had a maternity leave in both of my churches. That is more common today, but it wasn't when I started. As I mentioned earlier, I started working at my home church because I was *filling* a maternity leave, so they had dealt with that process before. They learned a lot of things along the way, so I was well supported.

But there are lots of tricky questions that come with maternity leave as a pastor. Of course there's the need to fill your position for a year, or sometimes now for eighteen months. There are questions around whether you should be part of the process of finding someone for that role. And what will your involvement look like while you're on maternity leave? What are the expectations of you? Is there an expectation that you will still attend and be part of things, or is there an expectation you'll give space for that new person filling your role?

Navigating all of that was a lot of fun. In my first maternity leave experience, I did try to stay fairly involved. We remained connected to that community, and I hope it was helpful for the woman covering my position that I was around to answer some questions. But I was also really careful to point people to her as the new leader in that role. In my second church, when I took maternity leave, I gave a little bit more space—although my older daughter was almost four at that time, and she loved church and didn't want to miss it. I also still wanted to be connected.

It's tricky, because pastoral ministry is so deeply personal, and those relationships are significant. You're not just clocking hours and filling a job—church life is part of your family. I don't think there's a cookie-cutter way to do maternity leave right, and I think it looks different for everyone. But you need to make sure that expectations are clear: for you as the pastor, for your family, and also for your church family. Make sure those expectations are well communicated so that people aren't disappointed or hurt, and so there's an idea around when you might return, if that is the road ahead.

Having those two maternity leave years was actually really helpful for me, because they allowed me to step back from my work at the church. I was ready to have a break—not that maternity leave is a break in any way, but certainly I was done with being nine months pregnant and setting up chairs time and again.

Sometimes when things are so close right in front of you, you don't have the big picture. Life in ministry is so busy that you just go through your to-do lists and all the things that need to get done and the people who need to be cared for. You don't often have the time to step back and breathe and really look at the bigger picture of what's going on. So I found that maternity leave was really life-giving that way. I was able to ponder a bigger picture—to think longer term, and more strategically, and wrestle with some questions. I was able to do a bit of reading, and listen to a few podcasts here and there, and chat with other colleagues, and take a little bit of space. I enjoyed visiting other churches from time to time as well, to see what else was going on.

I mean, I had gone to church my whole life. And so when I embarked on my maternity leave, I learned that people *jog* on Sunday mornings. And people go for brunch on Sunday mornings. There was this whole world I had not been part of, and I found it fascinating! It was great to get out of the church for a little bit and take my baby to the gym or a swimming class or a walk in the park, and meet people from different walks of life who I otherwise wouldn't have had a chance to connect with.

WOMEN CAN'T CARRY IT ALL

I went through a divorce in 2018. And so, as a single parent, having my daughters the majority of the time—if I'm honest, it's really not easy to manage. Balance is a bit of a dream.

But I think life comes in seasons. Sometimes there are heavy demands—like in my work currently, there's lots of travel, which I really love. But then there are seasons with a slower pace. I get to work from home when I'm not travelling, and at home there's lots of quiet moments and I have more control over my schedule. Hopefully, maybe, those seasons balance out somewhere. But I wouldn't say that week-to-week it feels very balanced. The to-do list is never done; there is always something else. And so I've learned to ask: *What can I uniquely do? And what can others do just as well as (or most likely better than) I can?* I've learned to ask for help, which is really hard for me as someone who was raised to be independent. Some days, it really does just look like surviving and getting to bedtime.

I don't think that's a struggle that's unique to ministry. My generation in general struggles with always being "on" and always being available. We're maybe the first generation that can sort of take all their work home and be available to work all of the time. I think that is true across many sectors.

There are a lot of images or definitions one might have in relation to the word "feminism." If we're working with just a simple definition that feminism is about all genders having equal rights and opportunities, I would wholeheartedly agree. All people are called to join in what God is up to, both locally and globally. But if I have a criticism of the feminist movement, it would be that the role of women wasn't redefined—it was just expanded. And so women are often carrying way too much, managing homes and families on top of also managing careers. Society was like, "Oh, you want a career? Totally. We'll add that. What else do you want? We can add that too. How much can you handle?" You see women cracking because they just can't carry it all.

My mom would've been in the first generation of women who had a career. I saw her doing everything. It wasn't like she could focus on her career—she did all the cleaning and cooking and child-rearing and carried all the mental load of managing what a family looks like. I had a great dad, but that was new for him too, and he wouldn't have seen balance modelled in his life growing up.

I see some women my age who've gone back to trying to have a family that looks like their grandparents' generation, because they watched their mothers struggle under the weight of all this and were like, "I'm not doing it. We're going back to one parent working and one parent at home." But the trouble is, it's so hard financially in our culture today. Doing that means a lot of sacrifices.

There is a place for growth in this area, in society and also in church culture. We need to create more balance so that both men and women can flourish. I know what it looks like when we're *not* doing that: it looks like assumptions about gender roles, and still thinking of families in a traditional 1950s setting. That's just not what the world is like today. Families look so different.

WE ARE RICHER TOGETHER

Being a woman in ministry, I love being able to tell people what I do, just to see their shock! I'm a bit older now, but when I was ordained in my late twenties, I certainly didn't fit the mould of what people expected when you said "minister" or "pastor." And so that opened all kinds of doors. I was able to talk with people about the reality of what it means to be part of Christian community, and what leadership in churches looks like today, compared to what they'd known from past years.

But I think the greatest joy for me has been working together with *both* men and women. At the two churches where I pastored, there were always men and women on staff. I really appreciated the collaboration and the different perspectives that allows. With my work at CBM, it's the same. We have an incredible staff that shares deep respect for each other, with grace and humility. There are so many advocates for women in ministry there. So I've always seen and appreciated the impact and beauty of when men and women can serve alongside each other.

Earlier this year, I attended the assembly for the Canadian Baptists of Ontario and Quebec (CBOQ), during which they voted in their first female executive minister. It was a gift to be in that room for such a historical event and hear their excitement. Then just a couple months later, Renée MacVicar was appointed the first female executive minister for the CBAC. That was such a hopeful occasion—although if I'm honest, it was a tough conversation to sit through. There were difficult moments, when words were not spoken in love and care. I'm glad that people were able to share openly, but I was also very appreciative of the many men who came up afterwards to us women, wanting to make sure we were OK. They recognized that some of the conversation was really hard to listen to.

It's important that we're OK with our differences. For my brothers and sisters in Christ who land somewhere different theologically than me, I am grateful we can continue to work together. As long as we can do these things in love and grace, that covers a multitude of differences—and I really believe we are richer together.

My encouragement to women in ministry is to find peace in your calling. As I shared, your calling doesn't have to be some big "burning bush" experience. But find peace in knowing that you *are* called. We don't choose this; we are called to it.

God calls you *into* ministries, and he calls you out of ministries. On those days when it's really hard, I have found it helpful to know that I was called to *that* place at *that* time. Know when your time is up in a specific place and then go boldly to the new spot where God might be calling you. Maybe God will call you out of "vocational ministry" into something else. If he does, know that you are still called in that, too. We are *all* called. Listen to his still, small voice, and find peace in that.

Louise Hannem
Interviewed December 6, 2023

QUESTIONS FOR DISCUSSION AND REFLECTION

1. Louise recalls her earliest experiences of church with fondness. How did your early experiences of church shape you? What do you think young people in your church are internalizing from *their* experiences?
2. Maternity leave was complex for Louise to navigate as a pastor, but she describes it as life-giving. Has your church ever had a pastor go on maternity or paternity leave? Do you see that as different from taking a sabbatical?
3. Louise is honest about the challenges of juggling ministry and single parenting, especially as someone who was raised to be independent. Why is asking others for help so difficult? How could our communities better support exhausted caregivers?

4. Through her work with Canadian Baptist Ministries, Louise has found that partnership does not require uniformity, but rather a shared commitment to core values. As Christians, how can we partner well with those who hold different theological, political, or cultural perspectives? What opportunities and challenges exist in that kind of partnership?

12

Joyce Ross

Joyce was ordained in 2014 at the age of seventy-five. In this chapter, she describes her lifetime of experience in both prison ministry and early childhood education, vital community work in East Preston, Nova Scotia, for which she was awarded the Order of Canada in 2002. Joyce also describes her experience as a senior adult seminary student and her pastoral ministry internship at Stevens Road Baptist Church.

MY NAME IS REV. DR. JOYCE ROSS, C.M. (Member of the Order of Canada). In 1939, I was delivered by a midwife in the community of East Preston, Nova Scotia.

I am a Baptist by faith. I had a teacher in school when I was in grade two who did devotions in the morning. And she always talked about missionaries, so I always said I wanted to be a missionary when I grew up.

But at the age of nine, I had a heart murmur. The doctor told my parents that my heart was so bad, I would never live to be a teenager. But I believe in the power of prayer because I'm a walking miracle: my family was walking around my room praying while I was laying there in a coma for three days. Back in those days, you were laid out at home, and my father was making preparations to lay me out. But when they came to the room where I was, he said, "She's not dead—she's still warm."

So back to the doctor I went. And they thought I was dead, but I could hear everything that was going on the entire time. I could hear my family praying for me. And their prayers were answered and a miracle was performed, because when I got married at twenty-one, the doctor said there was nothing wrong with my heart. I know God's healing power performed a miracle over my heart, and to this day, I don't have anything wrong.

I got baptized in 1953 at the age of fourteen. Then our Sunday school superintendent at East Preston United Baptist Church asked if I would help with the toddlers. So that was my start in church ministry; my work began then and it never stopped. I taught Sunday school for over sixty-five years.

After I started teaching, the youth group lowered its age limit. The people who were leading the group asked if I would consider being a leader. So I had to pray about that, until God let me realize that this was a task he wanted me to do. I started that young people's group in the church with nine young people, and I ended up finishing in my role about five years later with eighty-four youths being active.

I felt that God was calling me to do more in my life, but then I ended up getting married at twenty-one and that calling didn't materialize. I'm a person that likes to take care of my home first: God is number one, and second is my family. So I always made sure that my family's needs were met before I went out to do something for someone else.

My mother always taught us that charity begins at home. I remember once I had an uncle come on a Thursday, and I offered him a cup of tea and a piece of apple pie. And he knew how busy I'd been, so he asked, "Where do you get the time to bake? It's Thursday and you're giving me pie." I said, "Uncle, my cupboard is always full. If I have to stay up late at night, I make sure that I have what my husband and children need."

God has shown me that if you're going to serve well, you've got to take care of your family first. What good would it be for me to go out doing for everybody else and leave my home work undone?

My pastor for many years was Rev. Donald Skeir, and he always told me I'd make a good politician. I said, "No, I'm married. I can't do that because that takes too much time away from my family." But I organized and built a building for early childhood education and worked at it for thirty-six years. I also did prison ministry in and out of the prisons for thirty-eight years, though I never had a prison ministry diploma. It is a gift from God that causes me to do this work and be so successful at it.

I NEVER SAY *I CAN'T*

My husband passed away the same year that I retired from early childhood education, so I decided I would go to Acadia Divinity College because they were offering a course in prison ministry. I thought, "When these chaplains leave the prisons I'm working with and another chaplain comes, they may look at me and ask where my papers are, and I don't have anything to show." So I went to the college and was interviewed, and they said I had to take the Bachelor of Theology or the Master of Divinity in order to obtain the diploma.

I never say *I can't*. I always tell people: I don't accept *I can't*. If you try and you fail, *then* you know you can't.

So I said, "At sixty-five years old, going to university . . . I don't think that's my cup of tea. But I will go home and pray, and if God wants me here, he'll send me back." And that he did. He answered my prayer.

And when I enrolled in 2005, I said, "Four years—I don't know, that's a bit much at my age, but I'll try it." So I took courses in evangelism and the Old Testament. And for my first exam in evangelism, I got an A plus. So they enrolled me in the Master of Divinity program.

Well, I did that for one year. Then they were talking about getting a second language—you can't graduate with the MDiv if you don't take Greek or Hebrew. I went down to the secretary and said, "I am not prepared to take a second language at my age, so I guess I'll have to give this up." And she said, "No, you can take the BTh, and then it's not required to have a second language to graduate."

So I demoted myself. I was not going through all of that just to get a prison ministry diploma! I started the following year in the BTh.

I was blessed at Acadia, and the students and teaching staff were excellent. When I walked in the first day, I guess they saw that I was older and they said, "Don't worry—there was somebody in Japan who just graduated with a master's degree at ninety-two years old!" So they said, "You don't have a problem—you can do it."

A couple of times, snowstorms were coming up and they would say to me, "If the snow starts, you're not going home. So always carry an overnight bag in your car because you can stay with us." So I stayed at a couple of students' homes, and they were very encouraging.

I completed my work, but I did not want to be ordained as a pastor; God called me to be out in the field, working in outreach ministry. At graduation, Dr. Harry Gardner asked me why I didn't want to be ordained. I told him I didn't want to be a minister preaching in a church because that confines me. He said, "But you did the work. So if you did the work, I feel that I'm going to recommend you to the committee that will have to interview you. And if you pass that, then I recommend you be ordained." And that he did.

STEVENS ROAD BAPTIST CHURCH

I went to the committee. And all the things I'd heard about preparing for the examining council, and how tough and how hard it was—it wasn't for me. I went with God on my side, and his grace and mercy. I went, and I'm still waiting for them to ask me the tough questions that I couldn't answer. I went through with flying colours.

So they said all I'd have to do is an internship for a year at a church.

Following that interview, I was at another workshop meeting. This pastor asked me how I was doing and I said, "I'm doing great! They recommended me for ordination. I passed the test. And they told me I have to do a one-year internship at a church." And the pastor said, "You can come to my church!"

She took it back to her congregation and let me know I could go there. That pastor was Shirley DeMerchant,[1] of Stevens Road Baptist Church. And that was a White church, but God is colourblind. He does not choose us by our colour. So I went and I served there for a year.

It was an excellent time. I knew everything about the church, inside and out. They took me to every committee meeting, every church meeting, and all those specific groups like the missionary groups and the finance committee—I attended everything. I preached there many times. And even after I left, a couple of families asked me to do funerals. So they treated me well and involved me in everything. I'm actually still a member of their women's missionary group—I never left it, because I enjoyed it so much and we

1. See chapter 6.

don't have a missionary group in my church. I love the work of the missionary and I thought, "This is as close as I'll get!"

I told them when I first got there how I always had a desire to go on an overseas mission. So during my time, a chance came up for me to go on a short-term trip, and they provided half of the money for me to go. But I was sick for a while, so I didn't accept it because I didn't want to go that far away while sick. That was as close as I came to getting my wish. I guess it wasn't God's plan for me to go—but that's how good they were to me at that church.

THE INMATES I WORKED WITH

After thirty-eight years, I'm still with the prison ministry.

I've been in every institution in Nova Scotia, as well as in New Brunswick—even to Dorchester.[2] The chaplains used to always call me when prisoners got in trouble and ask if I'd come talk to them. So I would go and talk to them, and when I got home, the chaplains would call and say, "Well, what did you do? What did you say?" Because the inmates' total attitude had changed. I'd say that I didn't have a chance to say anything—I just listened. The inmates just needed somebody to listen.

Once, I was travelling with a group to Dorchester, and it was storming. I had three carloads with me and didn't realize how bad it was going to be. The cars in front of me started slowing down, so I'd pass them and speed up a little bit so we could move. When we got to Dorchester, one of the other drivers said, "You were driving too fast! Didn't you realize the roads were icy?" And I said, "Well, no, I didn't, but God slid me right on in!"

Some of the inmates I worked with gave their hearts to the Lord in prison and then came out and got baptized. I told one of those young prisoners, "I'm not here to choose the church you go to. I'm here to give you the Word of God. Wherever you feel comfortable going, that's your choice."

2. Dorchester Penitentiary.

So he chose to go to another church, but he asked me to stand beside him while he gave his testimony at his baptism. So I called his pastor and explained what had happened in prison and what this man's request was, and the pastor had no problem with it. Then while the young man was preparing for baptism, he said, "I want you to carry my blanket to the pool, and I want you to sit beside me."

See, when you go to the water to get baptized and you come up, you're all soaking wet and it shows your body. So typically, your parents would go up to the pool and watch your baptism. Then they're right there with a blanket to wrap around you the minute you come out, and they have a towel to wipe the water off your face.

So I told this young man, "Now you're asking a big 'if.' That's your parents' job. I guess I have to get clearance from your parents."

So when I called the parents, the father said to me, "Joyce, what you did for that boy, in thirty-one years we couldn't do it." So when I got there, his parents were sitting in the seat behind him, and he was in the front seat with his blanket and towel, waiting for me. It was a great honour.

That was fifteen years ago, and we're still friends. When he gets down and something is not working right with him, he will always call me, for prayers. He said, "I don't know what it is, but whenever I'm down and lonely and I call you and we pray, there is just a total changed atmosphere. It just lifts my spirits."

Several times, he's come and brought me special gifts, and he'll take me out for a meal. And it's just a pleasure to have worked with this young man through his Christian experience.

CENTERED AROUND YOUNG PEOPLE

I didn't pastor a church until my home church's pastor resigned in 2019 and they asked if I would take over until they could get somebody else. So I filled in for two and a half years at East Preston United Baptist Church.

That church is 180 years old. The first female—and the first person—who was ever ordained in that church was me. We have other pastors from East Preston, but they got ordained in other churches. In 180 years, I was the first one who came up from the roots of that church and was ordained in that church.

And you know how Jesus was treated when he went to Bethlehem to heal in his own country? It just didn't work. He wasn't accepted, because they said, "He's just the carpenter's son." And he couldn't do things where he was born like he could do in other communities. He said, "A prophet is without honour amongst their own."[3] I found that to be true during my ministry with my own community. It was very, very difficult. It was challenging, but I said, "I will persevere, because I know that God put me here for a reason. So I will persevere."

In our community, we had a shooting. And at the funeral, the church was filled with young people. The person who had been killed was a friend of my grandson, so when the funeral was over, a truckload of young people came over to my house with my grandson. There were fifteen or sixteen of them. So they all got on the truck and I said, "I'll take a picture of you."

Then I gave them a little lesson and I told them about the tragedy. I said, "This young man was all of your guys' friend. And if you know anything, you need to come close. You are the ones who are going to solve this problem and fix it. And God has called all of you for a purpose—God has a purpose for all our lives. And I pray that those of you who don't know God will come to know him, and will try to work together to stop this violence."

I don't know what all else I said, but at the same time, they were taping me and I didn't know it. So then they put me on Facebook! This woman comes up to me and says, "I'm so proud of you. The message that you left to those young people was amazing." And I was like, "What message are you talking about?"

She said, "When you were talking to them on the back of the truck from your yard—they all said it was excellent." And they were so proud of me for being able to express my thoughts and

3. Paraphrased. See Matt 13:57 and Mark 6:4.

encouragement to the young people. But I said, "I guess from now on, cameras are everywhere!"

It's like my whole life has been centered around young people. I started in Sunday school. I ended up in early childhood education. And I still work with youth today. The youth feel that I'm a person they can come to and confide in and get the help that they need.

EAST PRESTON DAY CARE

The Order of Canada is given to a person who has made a major difference in the world, in society, and in the community. As a young person growing up, I made a tremendous change in our community.

We had no recreation centre or anything, so we got a group of young people together and we fundraised and built our East Preston Recreation Centre. And that is still going on strong, since 1966. Three extensions have been added to it. We have a wonderful basketball program and lots of things going on there.

Then when I was working as a community health aide in our Partridge River Elementary School, they found that out of ninety-eight children, fifty-six of them needed auxiliary and remedial help. I asked what that meant, and they said, "Well, there's a lot of things they don't know. They failed the IQ test. They don't know what a light switch is. They can't tell a spoon from a fork. They don't know a bench from a chair."

I said, "Come on—I don't accept that." And I said, "One thing you need to know is that these children come out of their home and have never been outside the home until they come to school. And I think it's very unfair that you should give them a city-oriented IQ test and expect them to pass." All those children needed was to be exposed to some early childhood education.

So I asked the principal for the names of some parents whose children were doing *really* well. Then I contacted five mothers and told them about the situation I was exposed to, and asked if they'd help me in getting something together to help those children.

We visited a community service, looking for financial support. The gentleman in charge that day said, "You must be crazy. Where do you think the money is going to come from to do such a task?" I said, "God tells us to ask and we shall receive." And he said, "Well, if you're so smart, you go out and get the building and the children, and then we'll subsidize them."

So I said, "Thank you very much, sir. We will, and we'll be back."

Myself and those other women campaigned the whole community. We asked everyone if they'd help us raise funds to get an early childhood education building. With that, we managed to raise enough money to buy an acre of land from a gentleman. He was so supportive of what we were doing that he sold us an acre for $500.

When we turned the sod that day, we had a dollar and eighty-six cents in the bank. But we had promises. So we went on the promises of God. And there were people in that crowd who said, "She'll never make it. Give it five months and it'll be gone." But they didn't know how we were praying and trusting in God.

We finished that building for $165,000, nine months later, debt-free—*debt-free*. And in 1974, the East Preston Daycare was founded.

And that's why I said that God never fails us. Now, I say to people, "Only someone that's crazy would go and start a building with no money." But we did, and we succeeded because it wasn't us. It was God's grace and mercy that brought us through it all.

"THE CHILDREN ARE TOO ADVANCED"

After we got the building there, we started taking children. We took them from six months to five years old. Taking children at six months helped a lot of young people who had babies and had to drop out of school—they were able to get back to school and finish their education and get jobs.

It helped the grandparents, too, to have time for themselves because they were babysitters for their grandchildren. They all gave us so much money because they said, "We just want our freedom!" And so our community stays close-knit, and the families stick together and help each other.

I got the five women who were with me enrolled in Early Childhood Education at the Nova Scotia Teachers College. Our goal was to teach the children. We were a not-for-profit organization with a board, and I was the executive director, overseeing everything.

When the board first set up the payroll, I was being paid $100 a week, and the janitor was being paid $125 a week. I don't know whether they chose this because the janitor was a man and they thought he should be making more than me, but it wasn't long until someone came onto our board from Labour Standards and said, "There's something wrong with this picture. You have to increase your executive director salary immediately."

After we got the daycare, our programs were so good that they went nationally and internationally. We expanded to a family resource centre and offered pre- and post-natal care, and we had VON[4] foot care. We had classes where people could learn how to use the computer and everything.

We had all these things going, and then one day, there were three White gentlemen and a White lady who came in. They were from the Department of Education and they wanted to speak with me. Now, we had fought for years to have them come to the community and they'd keep us waiting for months to meet. All of a sudden, they came with no appointment to see what we were doing, because they said the children who graduated from our daycare centre and went to the elementary school were *way* beyond any child in the school.

And they said, "The children are too advanced, and we would like you to draw back."

I said, "I don't think so."

Then the primary school teachers all came to visit the centre, to see what we were doing. They said, "You're beyond our classes."

4. Victoria Order of Nurses.

So they all learned from *us*: the people who "did not know how" and "did not have."

We took those little children on train trips and bus rides and took them to the airport. We exposed them to everything. And we put pictures on the wall to let them know that you can be *anything* you want to be. This year we'll be celebrating fifty years.

We have a doctor out of those groups of children. We have firemen and policemen. Anything that you name—whatever those children requested they would like to do, we exposed them to it. And I am so proud of the success of those kids.

JUST TO THINK ABOUT MOSES

So with all this taking place, and working with all levels of government, I was nominated to get the Order of Canada. I was baking one day when the senator called to let me know I was nominated and it would take some time for the committee to get in touch with me. Then the letter came, saying: *You are nominated for the Order of Canada and we're recommending to give it to you, if you will accept it.* And I just threw it in my mail basket because I thought it was a mistake.

Then my secretary came in, two days later, and she saw the address on the envelope. She said, "What is this?" And I said, "I think they've got the wrong person."

She said, "Joyce, you're crazy. You better answer that letter and accept it."

So I accepted it, and I'll never forget the day it was announced. I couldn't say anything about it until they put it on the radio. So there I was at work and the teachers were all running into the office and hugging me, saying, "Congratulations!" And I said, "For what?"

One asked, "How can you work today?" And then my grandson said to me, "Nanny, if that was me, I'd be driving up and down the road and I'd be tooting my horn letting everybody know that I received this Order!"

Then one of the nurses who was teaching at Dalhousie University's nursing class put four classes together, which was over two hundred students. She got me to come and speak to them, to prepare them for outreach health work. And at the end of the class, she said to them, "My, what a lady! I don't know if we could accomplish what she did, and the things she's been doing to draw so many people's attention." She said, "We ought to give her an honorary nursing degree."

So about five years later, I got delivery mail again for this honorary doctorate. I said to my staff, "I guess I'm on the way out. God is taking me home to be with him, because this is just too much." That year I received *nine* honorary degrees.

I was recognized by the National Early Childhood Association, and our centre was considered the number one childcare centre in Canada. The government flew me to Honolulu, Hawaii, to talk to the people there about early childhood education.

So I thank God for the things he has brought me through, because I couldn't have done it without him. I'm eighty-four years old and I'm still busy and going forward. I just can't shut down. When he shuts me down, that's when I will shut down. God doesn't have any age barriers on what people can do.

Just to think about Moses: eighty years old when God chose Moses to be a leader. So we can't say that because of our age, we aren't able. Nothing is impossible when you trust God. So trust him, and go for it.

Joyce Ross
Interviewed March 6, 2024

QUESTIONS FOR DISCUSSION AND REFLECTION

1. What would be exciting or challenging about being ordained as a senior adult? Would you consider taking a new path at that age if God led you to?

2. Joyce explains that after the East Preston Daycare started thriving, several White government employees told her to “draw back.” How did racism contribute to the challenges faced by Joyce’s community? Where do you see racial inequality in your own context?
3. What part of Joyce’s story stood out most to you? Have you heard the stories of other older adults in your life? What stands out?
4. Joyce says her whole life “centered around young people.” What makes it harder to connect with young people as you get older? What are the benefits?

13

Jennifer Sutton

Jennifer was ordained in 2016 and has pastored congregations in Nova Scotia and New Brunswick, including Forest Hills and Aenon Baptist Church. In this chapter, Jennifer shares her story of coming to faith as an adult, and of the challenges she faced as a divorced single parent in ministry. She also describes her unique success doing community ministry through dance classes.

My name is Jennifer Sutton. I was born in 1967 in Oakville, Ontario.

My parents were Anglican, coming from England. They mainly went to church because my dad liked singing in the choir. But when I was around five years old, they stopped attending, so I also stopped attending church until I was an adult.

I moved to Nova Scotia and when I was around forty years old, I started thinking I should take my kids to church. Denomination wasn't really that important to me, but I went to an Anglican church first. Basically, I was bored to tears there, so I stopped trying and didn't go back. Then after I had my sixth kid, I was walking them all to school one day and we saw a sign for Vacation Bible School (VBS) at a local Baptist church. One of my sons asked what that was, so I told him it was a camp and he wanted to go.

Now, I had a dance studio across the street from a different Baptist church that was more fundamentalist. So all I knew about Baptists was that they didn't believe in dance, and I thought they were all nuts. I told my son with some disgust, "It's a *church* camp—and it's *Baptist*." But he still wanted to go.

So I phoned the church and asked how religious the whole thing was. The family pastor explained that there would be Bible stories and stuff. I asked if my kids were going to come home telling me I was going to hell because I didn't go to church, and her response was, "I hope not." So I signed them up for VBS.

By the end of the week, they'd had such a good time that I signed them up for Sunday school, and so I started taking them there. I went to the preschool class with my youngest, because that's about where I was faith-wise anyway. And then my daughter kicked me out of preschool because she didn't want me in class with her anymore, so I had to go to the grown-up service, which did not thrill me at all.

It was actually the preaching which really caught my attention, because I didn't understand any of it. But the pastor sounded so convicted by what he was talking about that it made me go read the Bible. I started attending regularly and took all the possible classes that were available: Bible studies, new member classes, and all that kind of stuff. At the end of my second time through a new believers' course, I was told that I was getting baptized. So I was baptized in August of 2010, and two weeks later, I was in seminary.

"I'M NEVER GOING TO BE ORDAINED!"

I went to seminary because I had run out of things to take at my church. My goal at the time was to get to know the Bible well enough that I could choreograph it for dance (though I never admitted that, because I thought I'd be slaughtered for heresy). I'd asked my pastor about taking one online course, which he said was garbage, so he told me to try auditing a course at Acadia Divinity College. I looked up their courses and there was one I couldn't pronounce about learning to interpret the Bible, so I thought, "Hey, what better course for a five-minute-old Christian to take?"

I signed up for that course in hermeneutics, and then the following semester I took two courses: one in Christian education and one in family counselling. By that point, I started feeling God calling me into ministry and I began working full-time towards a Bachelor of Theology. They say that God's timing is always slow, and I'm like, "Not always!" Sometimes you need to just hang on and go for the ride.

Evangelism was my jam. That was where everything clicked. My evangelism class started to connect all the dots for me, like how I'd be able to use dance and my faith and bring them together for ministry.

I'm usually slow on the uptake. When God's trying to tell me something, I think, "Nah, he can't be meaning that." I couldn't imagine why God would be calling me into ministry with my background. At the time, I was married to a non-believer, so that was causing a lot of struggles. I knew that wouldn't be helpful in trying to be called to a church, so I never imagined I was going to do pastoral ministry—I thought I'd be doing street ministry of some kind. I thought, "I'm never going to be ordained! I'm never going to work in a church. I don't need that." But my pastor kept saying, "You need to keep the doors open, because you don't know exactly where God is leading."

So I signed up for the ordination track of my program, but swore I'd never preach. At that time, I would throw up if I even had to say my name in front of the class. I couldn't speak in public at all. For my first preaching class (that I never ever wanted to take), my first sermon was on the second chapter of 1 Timothy.[1] I didn't know what that passage was about, and when I read it, I thought, "What the flipping heck am I supposed to do with this?" One professor gave me tons of research to read about different views on women in ministry, so that was a big help. That still keeps me in good stead when people comment on the subject and on the apostle Paul's writings.

Then Dr. Anna Robbins[2] started leading the college, which was also huge for me—not just because she was a woman coming into that position, but because she was so *normal.* The woman is brilliant, but as a friend of mine puts it, "Anna puts the cookies on the low shelf for us to understand." Anna has this bigger view of God and how he works. I remember that up until she started, I was afraid to say anything about evolution, because I thought I'd get in trouble. So she opened up the possibilities for me, making everything so much bigger, yet more accessible at the same time.

THE WORST EXPERIENCE OF MY LIFE

By the last semester of my BTh, my husband decided he wanted out of our marriage. Going through a divorce put a whole new spin on the ordination process. The first person I told was my pastor. Then I told the college, and then I had to contact convention. I met with them and they advised me how to proceed.

You usually have two interviews as part of the ordination process. You have an entrance interview during your first year of

1. First Timothy 2:11–15 instructs a woman to learn in "quietness" and not "assume authority" over a man (see NIV).

2. Anna Robbins was interviewed for *Called to Serve*. The episode is available at calledtoserve.ca and on Spotify and Apple Podcasts.

studies and then an exit interview in your last year. Well, I had *five* interviews. My first one went fine. Then I had another during my second year of studies, which I was told was normal in my circumstances because I was new to faith. That meeting was really encouraging. Then in my exit interview, they informed me that I would need one more brief check-in in May before going to the examining council in August.

That brief check-in blew apart. It was probably the worst experience of my life. What was supposed to be fifteen minutes turned into an hour and a half of grilling—it was just monumental bad stuff. I was pretty much put on hold, and at that point I decided I didn't want to continue anymore, because it wasn't worth it.

Soon afterwards, Renée MacVicar contacted me about a travel course in Prague for youth pastors. She assumed I had not bothered to apply because of finances, so she informed me there was one spot left and the cost was covered. God had been putting my name in her head when she prayed about it. I wasn't even aware of what the course was about, but she told me, "It's about artistry and ministry. You have to go."

So I flew with her to Europe, and she spent the whole flight telling me, "Jen, if you don't want to go forward for ordination because you feel God does not want you to be ordained and has other plans, that's one thing. But if you're not going forward with this because some men have stepped in and decided you're not allowed, then you're not following God's call."

When I returned home from Prague, I decided to follow through with the hoops that had been set up for me to jump through before I could proceed with ordination. Then I finally went forward to the examining council, which was an awesome experience. It was fun! What was really cool is that the night beforehand, I was listening to a piece of music, and God gave me the choreography for a dance about Sarah and Hagar. I choreographed it the night before I went into council, and that made me completely calm, because I had my mind on that.

YOUTH AND FAMILY MINISTRY

My ordination service was in 2016, at Windsor Baptist Church in Windsor, Nova Scotia. It was great. Anna preached, and I had my dancers perform the piece about Sarah and Hagar. And you know how in those ordination services, there's always a time for people to bring greetings? I hate that. I absolutely hate that part of the service, because it goes on forever and there's no memory of it afterwards. So I put up postal paper for a mural and set out colourful markers so everybody could write their greetings on the wall, and I still have that scroll.

I was called to Windsor Baptist for a new position they had just developed, called the "Pastor of Family Life." So I was the POFL. I had one service together with the lead pastor before he was called to another church, so then I was pastoring by myself.

Windsor had come up with a new vision statement, which was to be a congregation of Christ followers with an intentional outreach to youth and young families. So that was the focus of my job, but there was no senior pastor in place, and I was only part time. It was a wee bit of a challenge, and people were not keen. Some felt they should not have brought me on until they had a lead pastor in place, but they knew they'd lose their few families if they didn't call somebody.

I was there for three years, but I really needed to get a full-time position. So in 2017 I began pastoring in Wolfville, Nova Scotia, in a full-time role that was meant to be a co-leading position. But again, the lead pastor there was retiring just as I came in. I suggested the church call both positions at once so they could make sure they had a unified team, but they opted to bring me in first.

A year later, they called a senior pastor who was on a very different page from me. I'd been brought in to connect with the community, encouraging youth and families and outreach. The new pastor was very traditional and liturgical, so it didn't go that well. They tried to figure things out, but it would've ended up causing a split in the long run and I wasn't willing to do that.

At that time, I was contacted out of the blue by Forest Hills Baptist in Saint John, New Brunswick. They were creating a new pastoral position for children and families and were looking for somebody to develop that ministry in their church. So I accepted that call and moved to Saint John in the fall of 2019. Then the pandemic hit in March and I stayed for four years.

WHAT PEOPLE DON'T REALLY WANT TO SEE

After the pandemic, Aenon Baptist Church in Chester Basin, Nova Scotia, contacted me. I told them I wouldn't be available to move for a year, because my son was just entering grade twelve and I didn't want to move him during his last year of high school. The church opted to wait for me, and so in 2023 I was called there to a senior pastoral role.

There was no honeymoon phase. I have yet to experience a honeymoon phase at a church, because I generally have gone into newly created positions with a lower-than-usual acceptance rate. Some families left Aenon simply because of my gender. Churches will usually be accepting of a female if they aren't in a senior pastor role, but that position was solo, so I dealt with that.

However, I'd learned from previous experiences that while churches need to keep the identity of pastoral candidates a secret, some information about me had to be known ahead of time. I'd previously candidated for a church that was so good about keeping everything anonymous that the congregation had no idea I was a woman. I spent the first ten minutes of that meet and greet with everyone searching over my shoulder for my husband, the pastor. That experience didn't go well, because people were blown out of the water by the fact that I was female, and I was divorced.

So when I candidated with Aenon, I wrote a letter for the congregation to read two weeks before I came. It was actually very difficult to conceal my identity, because there's not too many single mothers of six kids who do dance in our convention, believe it or not. But I let them know I was female, and divorced, and had children, so they could process it and pray about it in advance.

I am exactly what people don't really want to see as a model for a church, but I am the reality of what our world is. And I can connect with the community on different levels. I know when I first started going to church, I didn't want to talk to our pastor because he was perfect. He's a very good friend of mine now, and I know he's *not* perfect, but there he was: a young guy, married, with two kids, a boy and a girl. You couldn't get any more picture-perfect, right? So I didn't think he'd be relatable.

Judith Tod, a retired female pastor whom I very much respect, even said to me that if she had seen my resume without knowing me, she'd have immediately assumed I wasn't able to do the ministry. Because as soon as a church sees you're a single parent, they wonder how you will have time. Yet there are single working parents in all sorts of fields who also end up spending their off-time volunteering at churches. It would be nice to have more understanding, but thinking single parents *can't* do ministry is not the answer.

Judith was an amazing mentor to me while I sought ordination and looked for a church. She was ordained herself when women were still struggling at examining council, fighting with the men in those meetings who'd refuse to vote on women. She is a warm, kind, beautiful person, with a backbone of steel when she needs it. She is also divorced, so she understood that whole aspect and was an incredible support to me.

PASTORING AS A SINGLE PARENT

There's still an underlying idea that if a woman is divorced, what did she do? The divorce wasn't even my choice. There's divorced men who are pastors, but they don't get the same level of suspicion. People are usually more like, "Oh, that poor guy. We need to help him out because here he is, and he has to look after his kids sometimes all on his own."

Even at the Divinity College, I had six kids as a single parent, and there was another woman there with four. And we had to do the same things as everybody else. I mean, the college was supportive, but there was no special treatment. Then they had a male student who was a single parent of one kid and it was like, "Oh, we need to make adaptations for him because he's a single dad." Like, what the heck?

As a pastor, I would never have gotten away with staying home because my kids needed me for something, or because I needed to go to doctor's appointments or whatever. But I've worked with men who are married with children, and they can take the time to do things like that and are congratulated for it. People think, "Look what great fathers they're being because they're invested in their kids' lives." Whereas if I had tried that, people would've said, "See, we knew that a single parent couldn't handle it."

It's often said that God calls you to be a parent first and a minister second. And I firmly believe that. But when ministry *is* your way of supporting your family, that puts a bit of a different spin on things. That's where the challenge was for me. My kids often suffered from my lack of availability, because ministry was my sole way of supporting them—other than dance teaching on the side. So I couldn't screw it up. If I messed up, then I couldn't support my family.

I incorporated my kids into what I did when I could. For example, if I was going away to Tidal Impact, CBAC's youth event, I'd take my kids with me. They could be involved in the children's programming when they were young, and as they got older, they became volunteers and helped serve at that. So that was how we worked it out for ourselves. But to be completely honest and fair, my children did suffer from my lack of being available as much as I would've liked.

REACHING THE COMMUNITY THROUGH DANCE

One thing that has been pretty cool throughout my ministry is I've been able to incorporate dance in various capacities. I have a separate ministry called Ministry in Motion, which I take with me everywhere. When I was in Wolfville, I taught dance full-time in addition to my work at the church. Those dancers were experienced and went to competitions, but they also danced for my ministry. We travelled all over the Atlantic provinces, including Newfoundland, teaching churches how to start their own dance ministries.

Originally, when I began dance ministry, I thought of it as a way for the audience to learn. I'd choreograph Scripture and theological pieces. But I realized that, actually, a lot of my dancers were unchurched girls, and they were coming to understand faith through dance. And their experience of church was really positive, because every time they went to a church, they were welcomed and celebrated. They were excited to read the biblical passages their dances were based on—they'd say, "I have to go read the Bible so I can dance this better."

When I went to Forest Hills in Saint John, I was able to have dance as part of my ministry at the church. So I offered free dance classes to kids in the community, and parents who might not have been able to afford that activity could have their kids try it out. I ended up forming a dance team, taking them to competition, and it was really exciting to see how that ministry created almost a second congregation at the church.

I started with dance, and then I did drama classes and "messy science" nights, and we had a discipleship night as well. There were options for kids every night of the week. I'd spend so many hours a week with them that I'd obviously get to know them far better than I would if I just saw them once at youth group. I'd also get to know their parents.

There wasn't a lot of support from the church leadership for this ministry because it "just" attracted girls. But it *didn't* just attract girls, because when you bring in little girls, you also bring in their dads. That demographic of men that we're losing in our churches and having such a struggle reaching were right there in the picture, bringing their kids to dance. Dance created an opportunity for the church to connect with them, disciple them, and point them to Jesus. Those dads were becoming involved and connecting with each other, and through the competitions and everything, they started to bond. They started helping each other out when they knew someone was struggling, and prayed for each other.

They even began volunteering for other ministries in the church. Sometimes they were intimidated because they weren't necessarily believers yet—or if they were, they weren't discipled. So they'd ask, "How do we come and help you if we don't even know the Bible ourselves?" And I'd say, "That's OK, because I'm bringing you in to do something you *do* know how to do. I'll lead the Bible part."

The vision for what I was doing wasn't really understood, which was frustrating. But it was also exciting because I could see what the possibilities were, even if other people could not. I know there are pastors who will go and minister to sports teams, and that is more recognized as ministry. But dance is something you can bring directly into the worship service. Not to put down sports ministry at all, but it's a little hard to play hockey during church on a Sunday morning! At the last recital I did for Forest Hills, I took a picture of all the dancers and their families on stage, and there were over a hundred people there. These were people who came multiple times during the week, and I ended up baptizing four kids who came to faith because of dance.

JESUS WAS A FEMINIST

Jesus gave the responsibility of preaching the gospel first to a woman. He knew she would get the job done. I think Jesus was a feminist himself—though I usually get a death glare when I mention that. But it's true: he lifted women up. He treated them as equals. He always gave them dignity and respect, regardless of their station in life, and empowered them. Feminism is a four-letter word in the church, but I don't think it's a bad thing—to me, it means equality. It's not about bashing men or raising women above men; it's about equal opportunities for both genders.

Last summer at Oasis, Renée MacVicar was voted in as executive minister for the CBAC, and if there's one thing I learned there, it's that we've come a long way. But we still have a long way to go. I was quite frightened by some of the comments and the anger level. I expected to hear some of that stuff, but I wasn't expecting the anger to be at the level it was. But Renée was amazing at handling it, and I was so encouraged to hear from many men who stood up in support of her—not because she was a woman, but in spite of the fact she was a woman. They weren't like, "Yay, we're going to have a woman leading our convention!" It was more like, "We're not going to put our foot on her back and prevent her from rising up to where she needs to be. We're going to encourage this *person* to do what God has called them to do, regardless of whether they are male or female."

If our churches could overall start looking at giftings instead of gender, I think we'd finally be on the right track of following the Holy Spirit. I did hear one woman speak about women in ministry in our convention, and she felt we hadn't gotten anywhere and weren't getting anywhere soon. I thought that was quite a depressing, negative view. I do think we've come a long way—we're on the right trajectory. And I think there's brighter days ahead for women in ministry.

If you're in ministry, gather around you a group of people who will pray for you and encourage you—people who will have your back, regardless of what happens within your ministry. For many pastors, that's a spouse who will always have their back regardless. But you need more than that. You need a village—a fortress on the rough days when you really need to know that this is where God has called you, and this is his plan and his purpose. Sometimes it's hard to remember that when you're getting the stuffing kicked out of you. Gather people around you who can lift you back up and say, "Nope, you're on. This is it. God's got you."

Jennifer Sutton
Interviewed November 24, 2023

QUESTIONS FOR DISCUSSION AND REFLECTION

1. Jennifer was initially drawn to seminary in order to deepen her creative expression through dance, and dance continued to be a powerful avenue for her ministry. Have you seen other examples of unconventional ministries being a blessing? How could you contribute your own areas of expertise to your church and community?
2. In Jennifer's experience, divorced women are perceived differently than divorced men. Have you seen double standards like this in church and society? How might we begin naming and changing them?
3. Although Jennifer heard one woman say there's been little progress for women in ministry, she felt more optimistic. Do you share her hope? Where have you seen signs of progress, and where are there still barriers that need to be changed?
4. The women in this book express a variety of perspectives on feminism and the feminist movement. Do you agree with Jennifer that feminism is a "four-letter word" in the church? How would you describe your own perspective on the feminist movement?

14

Hannah Bartlett

Hannah was ordained in 2021 at Cornerstone Baptist Church on Prince Edward Island, where she serves as the Next Generations Pastor. Her ordination marked the first time in the CBAC's history that the daughter of an ordained woman was ordained. In this chapter, Hannah shares her experience growing up in an environment that affirmed women in ministry and provided her with strong female mentors. She describes her team-based approach to next generation ministry, and explains how her husband's support enabled them to both pursue pastoral callings at their multi-site church.

My name is Hannah Bartlett, and my maiden name was Hannah Steeves. I was born in 1994 in Moncton, New Brunswick.

I grew up going to the Journey Church in Moncton, and my mother Carolyn Steeves was on staff during my childhood and teen years.[1] She has since returned to become their senior pastor, which is pretty cool.

I became a Christian really early in life. I think I was seven years old, and my mom was the one who baptized me. My siblings and I were involved in church to the degree that most pastors' kids are, if not a little bit more. And I loved being at church—it was my favourite place to be. I did just about everything you could do there before I was twenty years old. Like, I preached my first sermon when I was sixteen. I did kids' ministry and youth ministry. I wrote plays that the church actually performed—which is very embarrassing when I think about it now, but I thought that was normal. I did outreach and tech stuff, and learned the bass well enough to play on the worship team. (I have not retained that skill.)

And so I just found myself on the pastoral ministry track—not with one defining moment, but that's where my whole life was headed and I didn't want to get off the train. If there *was* a defining moment, I think it would have been in grade eleven, when I worked at Camp Tulakadik in Norton, New Brunswick. I spent the days of that summer studying the Bible and worshipping and building relationships with kids, helping them come to Christ. And honestly, at the end of the week, I'd forget I was getting a paycheque. I don't want to say that too loud, but they'd come around with the cheques and I'd be like, "Oh, right. I would do this without getting paid!"

I got to be mentored closely by my church's next generations pastor, Jen McWilliams.[2] She had the mindset that if someone has a gifting, they should be using it—it doesn't matter how old they are. Mostly thanks to Jen, I was leading junior high by the time I

1. Carolyn Steeves was interviewed for *Called to Serve*. The episode is available at calledtoserve.ca and on Spotify and Apple Podcasts.

2. Jennifer McWilliams was interviewed for *Called to Serve*. The episode is available at calledtoserve.ca and on Spotify and Apple Podcasts.

was in high school, and then I was leading the high school youth group by the time I was in university. When I was serving at the church, she made me feel like I was a mini pastor. She was so good at handing over the keys. I remember going with her to conferences and people would ask her, "How is your teaching series going?" And she'd say, "Actually, you know what? I think Hannah is a better teacher than me. I'll let her answer that."

As a student, I'm sitting there going, "*What?*" It gave me such confidence to realize: *Oh my goodness, I can do this.*

HARD WORK HAS BEEN DONE

Growing up, I was blessed because I never really knew that the "women in ministry" thing was an issue. If there were people around me who thought that women shouldn't be in ministry, they never said it—at least not to my face! The only time gender came up was when I told people I was a pastor's kid and they'd ask, "Who's your dad?" Besides having to correct them, I was fully unaware of the fact that there was even a "thing" about women in ministry.

It was awesome to grow up in that culture, and I owe a lot of that to the women who've gone before me who have done the work. As I've listened to their stories on the *Called to Serve* podcast, I feel honoured to be among them. It's a humbling cultural moment for me, realizing that hard work has been done so that I have been (for the most part) very well received as a woman in ministry.

I did my undergrad at Crandall University, and then went to Acadia Divinity College (ADC) for my MDiv, with a concentration in next generation ministry. ADC gave me a solid foundation in an environment where diversity was celebrated in the classroom and in our churches, and where you could wrestle with the big, important stuff. I think one of the most important skills I learned there was the art of good critical thinking—being able to see an issue or doctrine from the other angles you don't agree with. And that's very important in this conversation about women in ministry. It's while I was at ADC that I started to hear murmurings here and there about how gender was an issue for some people. People would ask me questions like, "So what do you think it's going to be like as a woman in ministry?" And I was like, "Well, what do you mean? I'm here to be a pastor, like everyone else."

Of course, with my mom being a pastor, I'd already been well versed in the Bible verses and what they really mean in their context and so on. But I think ADC was my first exposure to realizing there is a larger world out there, and maybe not every person or every church is going to hold the same stance.

CORNERSTONE BAPTIST CHURCH

My mentored ministry placement was at Cornerstone Baptist Church in Cornwall, PEI, where I now work. I arrived in the summer of 2018, and the senior pastor, Phil Woodworth, gave me the biggest sandbox to play in. It was crazy to me that he was like, "Just go do what you do." I thought, "Really? There's no five-step plan?" He was so patient with me, and the whole staff took a lot of hits on my behalf. They had a lot of grace for mistakes I made along the way and really encouraged me in my leadership. They have such a culture of humour—I've never laughed more than I have in the past seven years, and the culture around our staff table really does feel like family.

That being said, Cornerstone is also a church that would historically have been under the impression that women could not hold certain offices. They reevaluated their position on that, and so I'm the first female pastor on staff. As I interned with the church—knowing that the hope was I'd eventually be hired on—people had different reactions, of course. Some people were thrilled and they'd tell me, "I'm so glad there's going to be women on staff! I don't know if I could've stayed here if there wasn't one." And there were people who said, "If there *is* going to be a woman on staff, I don't think I can stay." And then there were people in the middle who were still in process, going, "I'm not sure how I feel about this."

So that's the dynamic at play. Since I started, I now have two women working under me, and there are six women on staff. It's really cool to have our big staff meetings now and to look around and realize, "This is equal. Which is what it should be."

NEXT GENERATION MINISTRIES

So I'm the Next Generations Pastor. What that looks like for me right now is overseeing everything at our church that involves people under eighteen years old. Cornerstone has a pretty large kids and youth ministry—right now there are around 300 to 350 youth under the age of eighteen. And I mention that for two reasons. First is to say that the scope is too big for me to do it all myself. And second is because there were people who told me, "You're not going to be able to work in a larger context as a woman in Atlantic Canada. You'll have to go to Ontario or something." And God was like, "Watch me." So it's really cool to be in this context because I do feel a calling to Atlantic Canada and to the larger church.

In my ministry right now, I say that I am a team builder and a cheerleader. Those are the two things I do to keep the ministry going. When I first started, it was me trying to figure out how all these things were going to run. Now, it's more that I meet with our wonderful children's staff and volunteers and get to encourage them. I get to help them with their personal growth, their spiritual growth, and their ministry growth as well. I watch them execute wonderful things and see them get flowers for that, which is awesome.

With our youth ministry, it looks like me pouring into and equipping our small group leaders and actually building youth band teams. So we have four or five different teams of students who are mentored by worship leaders, who circulate through on Friday nights. And we're building a teaching team—I don't do as many devotionals at youth anymore because we're training up young adults to preach at youth group, so that eventually they can preach on Sunday morning. One of the most rewarding things for me to see is my student teaching team be asked to preach, and hearing Phil say, "These ones are so good! Put them up there on a Sunday morning!"

It's so great for our congregation to hear and see young people doing this stuff. And I think that direction comes out of my own experience of being allowed to do ministry at a young age. I want to get other young people into ministry as well.

Of course, I do all the other things that fall under the category of "pastor" as well, when they are needed and applicable. But really, when I come into work, my goal is: how do I invest well in people and teams so that they can minister to the people God has called us to? Because if it were just me doing it, I would die.

PROUD TO BE A CBAC PASTOR

My experience at examining council was quite different because it happened during the COVID-19 pandemic. So it all took place online in 2021, which was actually really nice because I got to be in my own space and just sit at my kitchen table.

I'd heard stories from people saying that sometimes the council asks about women in ministry—well, they're not supposed to ask about that now, but in the past they have. Knowing that, my experience going through was very positive. It was nice to look at the Zoom screen and realize I knew most of those people. They were friendly faces, and a lot of them had encouraged me on my journey.

On the other hand, I could look and see some people I knew had a different stance. And that is kind of tricky, knowing that somebody is probably going to vote against you just because you're a woman. It puts you in a place of vulnerability to know you're facing that. But overall, it was a really good experience. It was balanced; it was fair. I was ordained in 2021, which is one of my favourite memories. It was one of those God moments, where I felt like, "This is such a good fit. I feel called to ministry, I feel called to this place, I really love these people—and this is where I get to serve."

I was so supported and affirmed by my church at Cornerstone, and our whole staff took part in the ordination service and planned it. They dubbed over songs with different lyrics to fit me and our content—they're just funny people. And Renée MacVicar was actually the speaker for it. She'd been on a long journey with me, mentoring me on and off through high school and university. I know that everyone already knows she's amazing, but she truly *is* amazing. When I'd go out with her, she would never end our meeting first, even though she had so much going on. I'd talk about everything I wanted to, and then she'd say, "What else is on your mind?"

I've always wanted to emulate that quality. I'm not always able to do that, but I want to give people that feeling of, "So, what else is happening? I'm not in a rush."

It was amazing to see Renée be voted in as the first female executive minister for the CBAC. I just wanted to sit on the side with my pom-poms and cheer. I heard so many people speaking about her competency and faithfulness and intelligence, and her being the perfect fit for this role. And it's so true—it doesn't matter if you're a man or a woman, she was the perfect person for the job. Her being voted in made me proud to be a CBAC pastor. We're moving into a different era, which is great.

Obviously it was also a hard day in some ways because we heard the perspectives of a minority who made it clear they couldn't vote for her. And you know, that does hurt. You're not supposed to take it personally, but it does hurt a little bit. Renée is one of those people who has poured into me, and my mom was there too, so I was thinking about her.

One thing I can remember was stepping out of the room for a little break after all of the discussion, and Phil—my boss, my senior pastor—was waiting for me in the hallway, crying. And he gave me a hug and said, "I'm so sorry that you had to hear that." That stuck with me, knowing that he is behind me all the way.

THE REPRESENTATIVE OF ALL WOMANKIND

It can be hard to find female pastors to connect with. I know that's true for those in senior pastoral leadership, but it's also weirdly true in youth pastoral leadership as well. Children's pastors are typically women, but youth pastors are usually younger guys. So there's just a different culture where you feel like you don't quite fit when you're talking with them. I tend to feel like we're speaking a bit of a different language, or just having a different life experience.

One of the challenges for women in ministry is that most women are probably pioneers in their positions. So you're going to be the first example that people see. And honestly, I've been wrestling recently with something God has been saying to me—that it's not my job to do everything at the church just so other people can see a woman doing it. That expectation has not come from the leadership at all—that is pressure I've put on myself. I think: *Well, people need to see me preach. People need to see me in the service regularly. People need to see me doing X, Y, and Z because they need to see a female pastor doing it.* For some reason, at some point along the way, I decided that I need to be the representative of all womankind at Cornerstone.

We obviously do need women's voices in all those areas. But what *I* really need to do is settle into where God has called *me*, right now. And that's not to everything that a pastor *could* do—it's to what God has called me, Hannah, to do. It's such a relief to realize that God has a specific call on your life for this season. You don't have to do it all. God will put the right people in those places. If I think I have to own everything, that means there's a bunch of women out there who will never do it.

MINISTERING AS A COUPLE

As I've listened to the stories of other female pastors, I've heard so many women praise their husbands, and I'm right along there with them. My husband John is amazing. He made the call in our marriage to say, "You're going to go first. You're going to get your MDiv first. You're doing examining council first. Let's get your career on the road so that, in case a baby does come along, you will be far enough that it's not necessarily going to derail you for years." He sacrificed a lot to make sure that I could be full-time at school, and he followed me to Cornerstone, where he now also works. I so appreciate his heart and his mentality to say, "I understand that for a woman, it might be harder to do those things later. So why don't you go first?"

So now we're both doing ministry full time together. He is at Cornerstone's Stratford site, and I'm at the Cornwall site. It's a nice little "marriage" of our roles: we're working at the same church, but in two different congregations. God's working in two different ways. And we love it. I know a lot of couples can work very closely together, but for us, that's not the healthiest.

Ministering as a couple comes with its own set of challenges and dynamics, for sure. But one of my favourite things is that we get to take our days off together. We get to schedule our weeks around the ministry, but around each other as well. It's been so life-giving for us to be able to have a sabbath together and bring to God a lot of the same things.

THE JESUS MOVEMENT

People would define feminism in different ways. For me, I'd say it's the idea that men and women are equally gifted and chosen by God to do what God has called them to do. I mean, when we talk about the feminist movement—I think it's like a vehicle that God can use to get us on the *Jesus* movement. The feminist movement is never going to solve the problem of sin in our lives, even though God can use it and say, "In this cultural moment, I can use this for my own purposes to establish that men and women are equal." But for myself, what's even more important is the Jesus movement—the Jesus way. It's only the Jesus movement that's truly going to get us to be men and women both reflecting the image of God.

I used to struggle with impatience for people who are still processing this issue. But you can't live in that space. You have to be OK with working alongside people who have a different perspective than yours, or who are wrestling with it for the sake of the gospel. I'd hear people say to me, "I don't know if women can be pastors, but I think *you* should be a pastor." That would drive me a little crazy, because I'm like, "Well, I don't know how you reconcile that."

But I feel like the Holy Spirit has done a work in my heart to say, "Hannah, I am so patient with *you*. You need to have patience to let people process this through. And even if people come to a point that is not your perspective, the kingdom moves forward, and you can move forward together." That is a hard and humbling place to land. But God's been softening my heart to be able to wait and see. I ask him for patience in my life, and I can wait and see what happens for these people as well.

Hannah Bartlett
Interviewed January 17, 2025

QUESTIONS FOR DISCUSSION AND REFLECTION

1. Hannah felt pressured to represent women in all areas of ministry so others could see a woman doing those roles. When have you stretched yourself too far in ministry or volunteering, out of a sense of duty or obligation? What signs help you determine what God has called you to for this specific season of your life?
2. Hannah describes herself as a "team builder" and "cheerleader." What is your leadership style? What do you appreciate about the leadership styles of your church's leaders?
3. Like other women in this book, Hannah describes both the positive and negative emotional impact of attending the CBAC vote for its first female executive minister. Why do you think it can be painful hearing Christians debate issues around women in ministry?
4. According to Hannah, "it's only the Jesus movement that's truly going to get us to be men and women both reflecting the image of God." What does it mean to be created in the

image of God? How does the world distort our identity as image-bearers, and how does Jesus encourage it?

APPENDIX

Women Interviewed for Called to Serve

WE INTERVIEWED AROUND ONE HUNDRED WOMEN for Called to Serve, including a few who chose to remain anonymous and are not listed below. Most of the women we interviewed were ordained by Atlantic Baptist churches. However, as the interviews progressed, we realized that stories of women serving in CBAC ministry who had *not* been ordained, or of CBAC women who were ordained elsewhere, were just as significant to record.

Interviews and podcast episodes were ongoing at the date of publication. To hear new interviews or find those listed below, please visit calledtoserve.ca or search for "Called to Serve" on Spotify and Apple Podcasts. Interviews on our website are tagged and searchable by name, ordination year, and ministry location.

Ordination Year	*Name*	*Summary of Interview*
1976	Ida Armstrong-Whitehouse	Ida pastored numerous churches and also served in hospital chaplaincy. She describes evolving attitudes towards women in ministry over her years of service.

Ordination Year	*Name*	*Summary of Interview*
1976	Elizabeth Legassie	Elizabeth ministered as pastor, counsellor, and teacher. She recounts her years of experience in both Atlantic Canada and Kenya, serving with Canadian Baptist Ministries.
1984	Carol Ann McGibbon	Carol Ann reflects on her pioneering leadership with urban ministries in Nova Scotia and Chicago. She describes her long-standing commitment to social justice and educational innovation across urban and cross-cultural contexts.
1984	Christine MacDormand	Christine describes forty years of ministry, including the financial and social challenges she faced serving as a single woman. She mentions influences beyond the Baptist tradition.
1985	Miriam Uhrstrom	Miriam shares her experience serving as part of a clergy couple and explains what studying music taught her about being a pastor.
1986	Kathryn (Kathy) Neily	Kathryn describes the challenges of balancing ministry with parenting and shares how she experienced God's healing firsthand.
1986	Sara Palmater	Sara recalls being present at the 1987 convention assembly, when the group voted on whether to continue allowing women to go before the examining council. She explains that she strategically avoided advocacy during that time, because it would be perceived negatively.
1987[1]	Marion Aretha Borden-Davis	Marion worked as an educator. She shares that her pursuit of ordination included facing racism, yet she found she was able to serve without being ordained.

1. Borden-Davis was granted a license to minister in 1987; she was not

Ordination Year	*Name*	*Summary of Interview*
1987	Sharon Budd	Sharon reflects on a long-term pastoral position, emphasizing that for her, ministry has been a very positive experience.
1987	Joyce Hancock	Joyce shares about her ministry to Brazilian youth living on the street, where she found there were advantages and challenges to serving as a single woman. She also describes her current work with NorthWind Family Ministries in Ontario.
1988	Ardythe Ashe	Ardythe shares her experience of coming to faith at the age of thirty-seven, the challenges of pastoring after the loss of her husband, and why going to the annual convention gathering was valuable to her.
1989	Judith Tod	Judith's ministry included pastoring, chaplaincy, and working with refugee families. She describes the challenges she faced as a woman entering ministry, including her experience at the examining council.
1989	Maxine Ashley	Maxine graduated with her MDiv in 1970 but became frustrated with the lack of ministry positions available for women. She worked at three theological schools and explains why she eventually pursued ordination.
1989	Elizabeth Waugh-Olmstead	Elizabeth reflects on the 1987 convention assembly, when the group voted on the question of women in ministry. She also describes what it was like to serve long-term as a single minister, before retiring and getting married in her sixties.

---

ordained.

Ordination Year	*Name*	*Summary of Interview*
1991	Barbara Cochran	Barbara has pastored her church for around thirty years. She describes the difficulties she faced at the beginning of her ministry journey and her experience leading through the COVID-19 pandemic.
1991	Lola Mather-Dyer	Lola reflects on her particular call to rural church ministry, the importance of serving through presence and listening, and her impressions of Josephine Kinley Moore, the first woman ordained in the CBAC.
1992	Michele Bland	Michele describes her call to international ministry and her experience pastoring as a woman in Hong Kong, where she moved in 1996.
1994	Heather McGregor	Heather describes her challenging experience going before the examining council, and the lasting contributions she made towards improving that experience for future ordination candidates.
1995	Barbara Fuller	Barbara shares how she tragically lost her husband and then served in ministry as a single mother. She discusses how her theology changed concerning women in ministry and describes her international experience in Moldova.
1995	Anna Robbins	Anna served as faculty at the London School of Theology before becoming president of Acadia Divinity College. She describes her pathway into ministry as a young woman, her experience with theological study and academic leadership, and how partnership with her husband enables her to live out her ministry call.

Ordination Year	*Name*	*Summary of Interview*
1995[2]	Carol Smith	Carol was called to prison ministry, then unexpectedly began a journey towards ordination as a single parent and mature student. She discusses her experience within Baptist, Presbyterian, and United churches, and the significance she sees in ecumenical ministry.
1996	Marilyn McCormick	Marilyn shares her experience with depression and its impact on her work. Her service included children's, youth, family, and music ministry, and she explains how she eventually gained a sense of certainty that she was called to serve.
1996	Barbara Putnam	Barbara describes the airplane disaster that first drew her into military chaplaincy. She shares highlights and challenges from her career, including her role in responding to 9/11, working in ecumenical and multi-faith environments, and listening to people's stories through Operation HONOUR.
1997	Shirley DeMerchant	Shirley describes her experience pastoring in South Korea for a decade, the importance of diverse team ministry, and how she's avoided making gender a divisive issue in church.
1997	Carol Anne Janzen	Carol Anne reflects on the influence of her Mennonite Brethren heritage, her experience with doctoral studies, and being a part of the faculty at Acadia Divinity College.
1997	Margo MacDougall	Margo served as a counsellor, probation officer, and pastor. She describes the sexism she faced serving in ministry as a single woman and her current focus on supporting wounded pastors.

2. Smith was not ordained by the CBAC but went through the ordination process.

Ordination Year	*Name*	*Summary of Interview*
1997	Gail Whalen-Dunn	Gail discusses how she balanced expectations around ministry and motherhood, and how she handled doubt when others questioned her ministry call.
1998	Marlene Pitman-Knowles	Marlene describes her reluctance to embrace ordained ministry, and the things she enjoyed most about being a lead pastor. She saw an increased openness to the idea of female pastors develop among both young and adult women.
1998	Joan Nickerson	Joan served as a chaplain at the Nova Institution for Women for over a decade. She shares the joys and challenges she found in prison ministry.
1999	Freda MacDonald	Freda came to faith as an adult in a military family. She shares her experience pastoring several churches, and describes the positive response she received to preaching as a woman.
1999	Robin McCoombs	Robin describes her journey to faith as an adult, her gradual call into ministry, and what it was like returning to a pastoral role after a difficult season of healing.
2001	Kimberly Beers	Kimberly worked in child protection services, at a crisis pregnancy centre, and in pastoral leadership. She describes serving alongside her husband, what true feminism looks like, and her calling to both motherhood and ministry.
2001	Audrey Carter	Audrey was ordained alongside her husband. She reflects on the advantages of team ministry and the ways she noticed being treated differently as a female pastor.

Ordination Year	*Name*	*Summary of Interview*
2001	Elizabeth (Liz) Johnson	Elizabeth was ordained at the age of sixty. She reflects on her community ministry and her service as a chaplain in assisted living. She also discusses the importance of listening in pastoral care, and her ministry emphasis on love.
2002	Nancy Draper	Nancy reflects on her intimidating experience at the examining council and the changes she's seen in Christian education over time. She describes her lifelong love of learning and her experience as a curriculum consultant.
2002	Heather Donovan	Heather describes her ministry with the Canadian Armed Forces, including the unique challenges and joys of military chaplaincy and her experience working with cross-denominational teams.
2002[3]	Rhonda Britton	Rhonda describes being called to ministry in her forties and how she went on to lead New Horizons Baptist Church through its historic name change. She emphasizes her ministry focus on ecumenical and community relationships, and how she identifies more with womanist theology than with feminism.
2003	Diane Juckes	Diane served as a pastor and as a chaplain for hospitals and correctional institutions. She describes ministry in a maximum-security setting, and the challenges and opportunities that come with navigating a multi-faith context.

3. Although she was not ordained by the CBAC, Britton's ministry has been significant in both the CBAC and the AUBA.

Ordination Year	*Name*	*Summary of Interview*
2003	June Keddy	June passed away in 2024. After serving as a caregiver, she felt called to ministry as a chaplain and pastor. She shared about learning the importance of self-care and the role forgiveness played in her life.
2003	Sherrolyn Riley	Sherrolyn entered seminary after retirement and describes persevering in ministry in spite of discouragement and depression. She also describes the differences between pastoring in predominantly White and Black congregations.
2004	Jennifer Varner	Jennifer reflects on a challenging church departure and describes what she gained from her years as a Baptist, before making the difficult decision to pastor in another denomination.
2005[4]	LeQuita Porter	LeQuita is a trained lawyer who pastored at East Preston United Baptist Church. She was the first female senior pastor in that church's 168-year-history. She describes the lessons she learned while seeking to balance ministry and motherhood, and her desire to empower women who have experienced abuse.
2005	Pamela Estey	Pamela describes her experience with music ministry, pastoral leadership, camp directing, and chaplaincy. She explains her current interest in addressing trauma in church settings, and muses on why she finds men and women tend to fall into different pastoral roles.
2005	Sarah Scott	Sarah shares how she approached differing opinions about women in ministry. She also talks about developing boundaries and how navigating motherhood shaped her call.

4. Porter was ordained in the United States.

Ordination Year	*Name*	*Summary of Interview*
2005	Maxine Gough	Maxine reflects on growing up in racially segregated communities and her experience as a second-career minister following a long career in education. She describes navigating racism, sexism, and ableism within society and church.
2005	Nancy Murphy	Nancy served as a children's pastor and describes her journey into becoming a single foster parent. She explains how her work in civil service is as much a ministry as pastoring.
2005	Sandra (Sandy) Sutherland	Sandra describes how her ministry identity slowly developed, from desiring to be a pastor's wife to becoming ordained herself. She also explains how she and her husband were able to manage being called to different ministries.
2006	Thelma MacDonald	Thelma pastored in several churches. She shares how she was called to ministry as a mature student and explains her passion for interim pastoring.
2006	Jennifer Riley	Jennifer talks about the different expectations faced by female pastors. She shares her impression of Oasis 2023, when Renée MacVicar was appointed executive minister for the Canadian Baptists of Atlantic Canada.
2007	Lois McLean	Lois reflects on her local church ministry across Atlantic Canada. She stresses the importance prayer has played throughout her life, as well as the significance of community during dark times. She also describes her special ministry with individuals and families facing death.

Ordination Year	*Name*	*Summary of Interview*
2007	Marlene Quinn	Marlene talks about her work with the Salvation Army and reflects on her experience serving in the community, including through the faith-based radio program she began.
2007	Virginia DeAdder	Virginia became a pastor after a long career in telecommunications. She describes wrestling with a call to ministry because of her gender. Although her faith began with an emphasis on fear, she shares how God has walked with her into becoming unafraid.
2008	Carol Dimock	Carol shares her experience serving in prison ministry and reflects on the transformation she saw in the lives of many men during her service.
2008	Sylvia Hagerman	Sylvia served in spiritual formation ministries and ministry to women. She talks about the challenge it was for her to navigate a call to ministry while being a mother, and how she has been able to treat any place like a mission field.
2009	Renée MacVicar	Renée serves as executive minister for the Canadian Baptists of Atlantic Canada. She is the first woman to serve the CBAC in this position. Renée describes her journey to faith and call to ministry. She shares about the importance of community engagement, and how play provides a taste of the kingdom of heaven.
2010	Sarah Clapham	Sarah has served as a pastor and hospital chaplain. She describes the importance of chaplaincy ministry and how she practices listening to the Holy Spirit.

Women Interviewed for Called to Serve

Ordination Year	*Name*	*Summary of Interview*
2010	Deb Stevens	Deb talks about receiving her call into ministry during a tumultuous time navigating a divorce. Since then, she has served as a pastor, chaplain, and social worker, and has developed a passion for small church ministry.
2011	Marion Jamer	Marion has served as a pastor and a community chaplain working alongside first responders. She describes her experience with the fire department and RCMP, and how she sees her ministry as that of an evangelist.
2012	Patty Beals	Patty shares her experience with rural pastoral ministry, in which she helped revitalize a small church. She describes performing around 130 funerals in her community and ministering to widows with empathy and presence.
2012	Louise Hannem	Louise discusses her experience taking maternity leave as a pastor, and the challenges of balancing ministry and single parenting. She also shares about her current work with Canadian Baptist Ministries, where she focuses on global mission and justice issues.
2012	Jennifer McWilliams	Jennifer describes growing up in the Salvation Army, her road to ordained ministry in the Baptist world, and the space she sees for feminism in church settings.
2014	Janet Kwantes Baker	Janet reflects on her ministry in several churches. She discusses leading an active rural youth ministry, and how it's possible for spouses to pastor in two separate congregations.

Ordination Year	*Name*	*Summary of Interview*
2014	Joyce Ross	Joyce shares her journey to ordination at the age of seventy-five. She describes her lifetime experience in prison ministry and early childhood education, vital community work for which she was awarded the Order of Canada.
2014	Carolyn Steeves	Carolyn talks about her experience working with multi-site churches, the impact of female role models, and her experience serving on the search team for the new CBAC executive minister.
2014	Sarah Stevens	Sarah reflects on coming to faith at the age of nineteen, leading a powerful youth ministry, and the ways that the COVID-19 pandemic affected her as a minister and a mother.
2016	Kristen Price	Kristen shares about her experience navigating shared pastoral positions with her husband, her heart for youth and children's ministry, and what it was like to lead her church through the COVID-19 pandemic.
2016	Jennifer Sutton	Jennifer shares her story of coming to faith as an adult, and of the challenges she faced as a divorced single parent in ministry. She also describes her unique success doing community ministry through dance classes.
2017	Linda DeMone	Linda describes how leaving an abusive marriage led her into ministry, and how she began a successful youth ministry at a declining church.
2017	Angela Wade	Angela reflects on her experience at the examining council, as well as the importance of maintaining balance to avoid burning out in ministry.
2018	Kayla Colford	Kayla talks about serving in military chaplaincy as a woman and the importance of knowing where her true identity lies.

Women Interviewed for Called to Serve

Ordination Year	*Name*	*Summary of Interview*
2018	Sarah Trenholm	Sarah talks about the pros and cons of serving as part of a clergy couple and gives her advice to women entering ministry.
2019	Andrea Anderson	Andrea is a former deputy minister in Nova Scotia's Public Service Commission, now pastoring at East Preston United Baptist Church. She describes how she was able to minister in her government workplace, and the experiences she had with racism in both seminary and public service.
2019	Ruth Tonn	Ruth was ordained following a twenty-year career as a semi-truck driver. She reflects on the difficulties she faced in securing a pastoral position, despite feeling a lifelong call to ministry and serving in churches extensively.
2019	Linda Perrin	Linda was ordained in her sixties, after a long career as a school principal. She talks about resisting her call to ministry, and how she leaned on God through sickness and continued finding ways to serve.
2020	Tammy Giffen	Tammy talks about the challenges she's faced navigating her denomination, in which leaders hold divergent views on women in ministry. She emphasizes the importance of mentoring upcoming female leaders, as well as not placing too much emphasis on one's pastoral identity.
2020	Rachel Kwan	Rachel shares her experience with music ministry, the challenge she had finding available ministry internship positions, and what it was like going before the examining council during the COVID-19 pandemic. She is the first ordained woman of Chinese descent in the CBAC.

Ordination Year	*Name*	*Summary of Interview*
2020	Melody Maxwell	Melody is the lead researcher for Called to Serve. She is a professor of Christian history at Acadia Divinity College. She shares her experience working in Christian higher education as a woman and the heart she's had to help female students in particular embrace their ministry calling.
2021	Hannah Bartlett	Hannah's ordination marked the first time in the CBAC's history that the daughter of an ordained woman was ordained. She shares her experience growing up in an environment that affirmed women in ministry. She also describes her team-based approach to next generation ministry, and explains how her husband's support enabled them to both pursue pastoral callings at their multi-site church.
2023	Kim Butler	Kim has served in worship ministry and senior pastor roles. She reflects on the effect of receiving the title of "pastor," and discusses how women can be pigeonholed into particular ministry roles.
2024	Sarah Cogswell	Sarah describes wrestling through being called to ministry as a woman and how she learned to embrace her limitations in order to avoid burnout and remain healthy in ministry.
2024	Sheila Cummings	Sheila was ordained after many decades of ministry service. She talks about ministering in the community, where she is known as the "arena pastor," and about the encouragement she received from numerous women who ministered without being ordained.

www.ingramcontent.com/pod-product-compliance
Lightning Source LLC
LaVergne TN
LVHW050630100826
845148LV00011B/1817

* 9 7 9 8 3 8 5 2 6 2 7 9 3 *